Title Page

Suspect by Default: Terror, Power & the Muslim Identity

A Constitutional, Investigative, and Human-Rights Inquiry

by

Fazal Abubakkar Esaf

Copyright Page

This book is a work of non-fiction based on documented cases, publicly available judgments, legal analysis, media reports, and human-rights research. While every effort has been made to ensure accuracy, the author does not claim infallibility. Opinions expressed are those of the author and are intended to encourage constitutional dialogue, legal reform, and democratic accountability.

This work does not endorse terrorism or violence of any kind. It critically examines counter-terror practices through the lens of law, civil liberties, and human dignity.

First Edition- 2026

Table of Contents

Dedication 1
Acknowledgement 2
Preface 3
Introduction 4
1: The Birth of the 'Permanent Suspect' 6
2: From Citizen to File Number 11
3: The Language of Terror 16
4: When Prevention Becomes Punishment 20
5: Media as the First Court 24
6: Fear as a Governance Tool 28
7: Intelligence Inputs 32
8: Profiling by Geography & Identity 36
9: The Informer Trap 40
10: Custodial Confessions & Coercion 44
11: Linking Unrelated Accused into One 'Module' 48
12: International Templates, Local Misuse 56
13: Poverty & Limited Legal Access 64
14: Lack of Awareness about Rights 71
15: Fear of Police = Self-Incrimination 78
16: Long Pre-Trial Detention 85
17: Family & Social Destruction 92
18: Social Stigma That Never Ends 99
19: Wrongful Arrests after Blasts 106
20: Confession-Only Cases 113
21: Youth Targeted for Online Activity 121
22: Families Who Fought Back 131
23: Political Capital of Terror Fear 138
24: Institutional Incentives 145
25: Media Ratings Economy 152
26: Silence of the Majority 159
27: Legal Safeguards First 166

28: Independent Review of Investigations 173
29: Hold actors accountable for wrongful prosecution 180
30: Media Ethics & Naming Protocols 187
31: Community Legal Literacy 194
32: Data Transparency 201
33: Reclaiming Citizenship 209
Conclusion: Justice, Rights, and Reform 216
About the Author 217

Dedication

To every family that waited outside prison gates for years,

to every mother who carried court documents like sacred texts,

to every child who learned the meaning of stigma before innocence,

and to every citizen who still believes
that justice must be stronger than fear.

Acknowledgement

This book would not exist without the courage of countless individuals who chose to speak despite fear—lawyers who fought decade-long cases without recognition, journalists who documented inconvenient truths, activists who preserved records when institutions failed, and families who refused to surrender to silence.

I acknowledge the contributions of human-rights defenders, legal scholars, retired judges, and independent researchers whose work laid the foundation for this inquiry. Many of them work without spotlight or protection, guided only by constitutional conscience.

I am grateful to those who shared their personal stories—often at great emotional cost—not for sympathy, but for accountability. Their resilience is the moral spine of this book.

Finally, I acknowledge every reader willing to engage with discomfort. Democracy requires not agreement, but attention.

Preface

This book was not written to defend a community.

It was written to defend the law.

Over the past two decades, terrorism has reshaped global politics, security doctrines, and public psychology. In the process, fear has become normalized, exceptional laws permanent, and suspicion institutionalized. While counter-terrorism is a legitimate and necessary function of the state, its execution has too often blurred the line between protection and persecution.

In many democracies—particularly in South Asia—Muslim identity has gradually shifted from citizenship to conditional belonging. The transition is subtle, bureaucratic, and rarely announced. It occurs through databases, intelligence inputs, preventive detention laws, media narratives, and prolonged trials that punish before judgment.

This book does not argue that terrorism is imaginary.

It argues that **collective suspicion is unconstitutional**.

By examining legal structures, investigative patterns, judicial observations, and lived experiences, this work seeks to answer a critical question:

Can a democracy remain democratic when one community is treated as a permanent suspect?

Introduction

In theory, the Constitution recognizes individuals.

In practice, security regimes often recognize identities.

Suspect by Default is an inquiry into how terror narratives, once introduced as emergency responses, become normalized tools of governance. It explores how Muslim citizens—particularly those from marginalized backgrounds—are disproportionately drawn into the machinery of suspicion, often without credible evidence, and held there for years through procedural delays, restrictive bail laws, and media stigmatization.

This book traces the lifecycle of suspicion:

- How names become files
- How neighborhoods become "zones"
- How preventive detention replaces investigation
- How trials outlast innocence
- How acquittal fails to restore dignity

Importantly, this is **not** an anti-state book.

It is a **pro-constitutional** one.

It acknowledges that law enforcement operates under immense pressure and that terrorism is real. But it also insists that **efficiency without accountability is dangerous**, and that **security without justice breeds alienation**—the very condition terrorism exploits.

Each section of the book builds systematically:

- From ideology to mechanism
- From arrest to aftermath
- From individual suffering to structural incentives
- From critique to reform

The ultimate argument is simple yet urgent:

A democracy that trades equality for expediency will lose both.

This book invites lawmakers, judges, journalists, students, and ordinary citizens to rethink how terror is fought—and at what cost.

1: The Birth of the 'Permanent Suspect'

How a global security mindset redefined Muslim identity as a default risk

The idea of the "permanent suspect" did not emerge overnight. It was not born out of a single law, a single speech, or even a single attack. It emerged gradually, through repetition, policy drift, and the normalization of fear. What began as an emergency response to extraordinary violence slowly hardened into a governing principle—one that reshaped how states perceive security, how institutions assess threat, and how entire communities are positioned within the architecture of suspicion.

After the attacks of September two thousand one, the world entered a new security era. The language of "war" was deliberately chosen: a War on Terror, undefined in geography, unlimited in time, and ambiguous in enemy description. Unlike conventional wars, this conflict was not against a state or an army. It was against an idea, a tactic, and—soon enough—an identity. In the absence of a clearly bounded adversary, states turned to pattern recognition, profiling, and preemption. This shift laid the foundation for a system where suspicion no longer required individualized evidence but could be inferred from association, belief, geography, or appearance.

The transformation was subtle but decisive. Terrorism was no longer treated solely as a criminal act to be investigated after the fact. It was reframed as a future possibility to be prevented in advance. Prevention, however, requires prediction. And prediction, when stripped of robust evidence, relies heavily on stereotypes, historical bias, and institutional convenience.

In this environment, Muslim identity became entangled with risk assessment.

This was not always explicit. Few official documents openly declared Muslims a threat. Instead, the association was built through layered assumptions: that extremist violence was primarily Islamic; that radicalization occurred within Muslim communities; that religious observance could be a marker of ideological danger; that Muslim-majority neighborhoods required exceptional surveillance. Over time, these assumptions hardened into operational doctrine.

The result was the birth of the "permanent suspect"—a citizen whose relationship with the state is mediated not by rights, but by risk.

In classical constitutional theory, suspicion is individualized. The state must justify why a particular person is investigated, arrested, or prosecuted. Post-9/11 security frameworks inverted this principle. Entire populations were placed under ambient suspicion, with individuals required to prove harmlessness rather than the state proving guilt. The presumption of innocence—once the cornerstone of democratic justice—was quietly diluted by the logic of precaution.

This shift was reinforced by international pressure. Global counter-terror frameworks, developed largely by Western security institutions, were exported worldwide with limited contextual adaptation. Intelligence-sharing agreements, terror-financing regulations, and watch list mechanisms were adopted wholesale by states with vastly different legal cultures and accountability structures. In many cases, these frameworks were implemented without adequate judicial oversight, transparency requirements, or mechanisms for redress.

What followed was a form of bureaucratic suspicion.

Names entered databases not through conviction, but through "inputs." Inputs could be based on anonymous tips, intercepted communications taken out of context, travel history, social media activity, or mere proximity to another suspect. Once entered, names rarely exited. The individual became a data point in an expanding web of suspicion—monitored, flagged, and revisited repeatedly, often without ever being informed.

For Muslim citizens, this created a parallel reality. Ordinary acts—attending religious lectures, donating to charities, traveling abroad, engaging in political speech—acquired a secondary meaning. Innocent behavior became legible as potential threat when filtered through the lens of counter-terror ideology. The same actions, when performed by non-Muslims, remained unremarkable.

This asymmetry is critical.

It demonstrates that the issue is not security itself, but selective suspicion. The permanent suspect is not defined by conduct alone, but by identity combined with conjecture. The burden of proof shifts imperceptibly: Muslims are asked, implicitly and explicitly, to demonstrate loyalty, moderation, and harmlessness in ways no other group is required to do.

Media narratives amplified this transformation. The language of terror reporting evolved into a vocabulary of presumption. Terms like "radicalized," "module," "sleeper cell," and "terror link" began appearing long before trials commenced, often before charges were even filed. Headlines became verdicts. Arrests were framed as breakthroughs. Acquittals, when they came years later, were treated as footnotes.

In this ecosystem, the Muslim suspect became a recurring character—interchangeable, abstract, and endlessly replicable. Individual stories dissolved into a collective caricature.

The psychological impact of this framing cannot be overstated. Communities internalized fear, mistrust, and self-censorship. Parents warned children to avoid public expression. Youth learned early that visibility carried risk. Legal consciousness was replaced by survival strategies. The relationship between citizen and state shifted from participation to avoidance.

From the state's perspective, the permanent suspect offered administrative convenience. Broad suspicion justified expansive powers. Preventive detention laws lowered evidentiary thresholds. Intelligence inputs became unchallengeable due to secrecy claims. Accountability was deferred in the name of urgency. Each successful arrest—regardless of eventual conviction—reinforced institutional incentives.

Yet this system contains a fundamental contradiction.

By conflating identity with threat, it undermines the very intelligence quality it claims to enhance. Overbroad suspicion floods agencies with noise, distracts from genuine leads, and erodes trust within communities that are crucial for effective counter-terrorism. Security professionals across jurisdictions have repeatedly acknowledged that community cooperation, not alienation, is the most reliable source of actionable intelligence.

The permanent suspect model does the opposite.

It replaces partnership with surveillance, dialogue with suspicion, and rights with discretion. It treats law not as a constraint on power, but as an obstacle to efficiency. Over time, this logic corrodes democratic legitimacy. When entire communities experience the state primarily through policing and prosecution, citizenship becomes conditional in practice, even if equal in theory.

Importantly, acknowledging this reality does not require denying the existence of terrorism or minimizing its victims. A human-rights–based analysis does not argue for inaction; it argues for precision. It insists that security measures be evidence-driven, proportionate, and reversible. It recognizes that exceptional powers, once normalized, rarely retract on their own.

The birth of the permanent suspect was not inevitable. It was the result of choices—policy choices, narrative choices, and legal choices—made under pressure and fear. Understanding its origins is essential, because systems born in crisis often outlive the crises that justified them.

This chapter does not seek to assign moral blame to individual officers or institutions. It seeks to expose a structural shift: from suspicion as an exception to suspicion as a default. From citizenship as a right to citizenship as a probationary status for some.

If democracy is to remain credible, this shift must be confronted.

Security cannot depend on identity. Prevention cannot override due process. And no community can be asked to carry the burden of collective guilt without eroding the constitutional fabric itself.

The permanent suspect is not merely a Muslim problem. It is a democratic one.

And its continued existence poses a question that every constitutional society must answer:

Can freedom survive when fear becomes policy?

2: From Citizen to File Number

How ordinary names enter intelligence databases

There is no ceremony when a citizen becomes a file. No knock on the door, no warning, no formal accusation. The transformation is administrative, silent, and almost always invisible to the person most affected. One day, an individual exists only as a name in civic records—voter lists, tax rolls, school registers. The next, that same name begins to circulate in intelligence systems, attached to codes, annotations, and risk markers. Citizenship remains on paper, but functionally, something has shifted.

In contemporary counter-terror frameworks, this shift is rarely the result of a single, verifiable act. More often, it is the outcome of accumulation—small, seemingly insignificant data points aggregated into a narrative of suspicion. A phone call logged. A journey recorded. A contact saved. A donation made. A message forwarded. None of these, in isolation, constitutes wrongdoing. Together, under the logic of preventive security, they can be enough.

This is how ordinary names enter intelligence databases.

Modern intelligence systems are designed less around crimes already committed and more around risks yet to materialize. This predictive orientation has redefined what counts as relevant information. Intelligence inputs no longer require the evidentiary rigor demanded in criminal courts. They operate under lower thresholds, justified by secrecy and urgency. The standard is not proof, but plausibility.

At the heart of this process is the "input"—a term deliberately vague. Inputs can originate from multiple sources: local police reports, intercepted communications, financial transaction alerts, immigration records, surveillance footage, informers, or foreign intelligence agencies. In many jurisdictions, even open-source material such as social media posts, attendance at public meetings, or religious sermons can be flagged and forwarded.

Crucially, inputs are rarely tested for accuracy at the point of entry.

An officer's suspicion, an informant's claim, or an algorithmic correlation can be sufficient to create a file. Once created, the file takes on a life of its own. It can be shared across agencies, duplicated across databases, and referenced in future assessments. Each reference strengthens its apparent legitimacy, even if the original basis was weak, speculative, or flawed.

This is how suspicion becomes self-reinforcing.

For Muslim citizens, the pathway from name to file is often shorter and steeper. Identity acts as a multiplier. Behaviors considered neutral for others acquire heightened significance when filtered through the lens of counter-terror profiling. Travel to certain regions, association with certain charities, or expression of certain political views may be interpreted as indicators of ideological alignment rather than constitutionally protected activity.

The individual is rarely informed of this transformation. There is no notification that one's name has been entered into a watch list, shared with intelligence units, or flagged for monitoring. There is usually no mechanism to challenge inclusion, no hearing, no opportunity to correct errors. The logic of secrecy overrides procedural fairness.

This absence of transparency creates a profound imbalance of power.

From a constitutional perspective, databases of suspicion occupy a grey zone. They are not criminal convictions, yet they produce real-world consequences. Being listed can trigger enhanced surveillance, repeated questioning, travel restrictions, denial of bail, or the invocation of preventive detention laws. In some cases, intelligence files quietly shape prosecutorial decisions, influencing whether charges are filed at all.

Yet because these files are classified, they remain shielded from judicial scrutiny.

Courts are often asked to defer to "confidential inputs" without access to their substance. Defense lawyers are told that disclosure would compromise national security. Judges, constrained by doctrine and precedent, may accept sealed material at face value. The accused is left to contest shadows.

This system fundamentally alters the meaning of due process.

Traditionally, the state bears the burden of justifying its actions through evidence that can be examined and challenged. Intelligence databases reverse this logic. They operate on trust—trust in agencies, trust in procedures, trust in the assumption that misuse is rare. But trust is not a legal safeguard. Without oversight, even well-intentioned systems drift toward abuse.

Investigative journalism across multiple democracies has repeatedly exposed the fallibility of such databases. Names added due to mistaken identity. Files created based on mistranslated conversations. Individuals flagged due to proximity rather than participation. Once inside the system, removal is difficult, sometimes impossible. Errors persist, amplified by repetition.

The human cost is substantial.

For those affected, life becomes a sequence of unexplained obstacles. Jobs are lost without explanation. Passports are delayed. Bank accounts are scrutinized. Police visits become routine. Each encounter reinforces a sense of permanent probation. Even family members may come under indirect scrutiny, widening the circle of impact.

Importantly, these outcomes occur without a finding of guilt.

From the state's viewpoint, intelligence databases are defended as necessary tools in an age of complex, decentralized threats. This argument cannot be dismissed lightly. Terror networks do exploit anonymity and informal connections. Early detection can save lives. The challenge, however, lies in distinguishing between targeted intelligence work and indiscriminate data hoarding.

When databases grow without restraint, precision is lost.

Security professionals acknowledge a phenomenon known as "information overload." Excessive data generates false positives, burying genuine threats under layers of noise. In such environments, identity-based shortcuts become tempting. Profiling replaces investigation. Risk assessment becomes guesswork.

This is where constitutional principles must reassert themselves.

A rights-respecting intelligence framework does not reject databases; it regulates them. It demands clear criteria for entry, periodic review, and independent oversight. It distinguishes between raw intelligence and actionable evidence. It ensures that inclusion is not permanent by default, but time-bound and revisable.

Several democratic jurisdictions have experimented with oversight mechanisms: parliamentary intelligence committees with real powers, independent inspectors general, judicial authorization for database inclusion, and limited disclosure to affected individuals once risks subside. These models demonstrate that secrecy and accountability are not mutually exclusive.

Another critical reform lies in auditability.

Every intelligence input should leave a trace: who entered it, on what basis, and for what purpose. Such audit trails deter misuse and enable retrospective accountability. They also protect officers by clarifying responsibility, rather than diffusing it across institutions.

Equally important is the separation between intelligence and prosecution. Intelligence should guide investigation, not substitute for evidence. Courts must resist the temptation to treat secret inputs as inherently reliable. The legitimacy of counter-terror efforts depends not only on effectiveness, but on fairness.

The journey from citizen to file number reveals a deeper truth: modern governance increasingly operates through data rather than dialogue. Individuals are reduced to profiles, probabilities, and patterns. When these abstractions intersect with historical prejudice, entire communities are rendered suspect by design.

Reversing this trend does not weaken security. It strengthens it.

A system that respects rights generates trust. Trust generates cooperation. Cooperation produces better intelligence. The alternative—a permanent database of suspicion—creates alienation, error, and injustice.

Ultimately, the question is not whether states need intelligence databases. They do. The question is whether democracies can ensure that such databases serve security without undermining citizenship itself.

When a name becomes a file without consent, knowledge, or recourse, democracy quietly loses something essential.

Restoring that balance is not a concession to extremism.

It is a commitment to constitutional integrity.

3: The Language of Terror

How words like "module," "sleeper cell," and "radicalized" become weapons

Language is never neutral in matters of power. In the realm of counter-terrorism, words do more than describe reality—they actively construct it. Long before evidence is tested in court or guilt is established through due process, language frames the accused, shapes public perception, and narrows the space for doubt. Certain terms, repeated often enough and without scrutiny, acquire an authority that exceeds their factual basis. They begin to function as verdicts rather than descriptors.

Among the most consequential of these are words such as *module, sleeper cell,* and *radicalized.*

At first glance, these terms appear technical, even scientific. They seem to belong to the domain of intelligence analysis rather than emotion or ideology. Yet their power lies precisely in this appearance of objectivity. When deployed by investigators, prosecutors, or the media, they compress complex human lives into simplified threat narratives. Once spoken, they are difficult to undo.

The term *module* is a case in point. In its original analytical sense, it refers to a structured operational unit within an organized network. In practice, however, it is often used retrospectively to bind together individuals who may have no proven operational relationship. Acquaintances, distant contacts, or even people connected through a single intermediary are grouped under a single label. The word performs an act of synthesis that evidence has not yet earned.

By calling a group a "terror module," investigators shift the legal terrain. Individual acts are no longer examined in isolation. Weak evidence against one accused is reinforced by the mere presence of others. Association substitutes for proof. The narrative becomes collective, even if the alleged acts are not.

This linguistic move is subtle, but its consequences are severe.

Similarly, the phrase *sleeper cell* carries a particular psychological weight. It suggests patience, deception, and hidden danger. A sleeper cell is, by definition, inactive yet perpetually threatening. The absence of action becomes part of the accusation. If nothing has happened, it is because the plan is dormant. This logic is nearly impossible to falsify.

From a legal standpoint, the concept creates a paradox. How does one disprove an intention that has not yet manifested? How does one defend against an allegation designed to exist outside time? Courts are often asked to accept the plausibility of future violence as justification for present punishment.

The language performs the work that evidence cannot.

Perhaps the most widely used and least defined term is *radicalized*. Unlike criminal categories, radicalization has no precise legal meaning. It operates as a psychological and ideological label rather than a juridical one. Its indicators are elastic: changes in dress, religious observance, online consumption, political opinions, or social circles. Behaviors protected under constitutional guarantees of expression and beliefs are reinterpreted as warning signs.

Radicalization discourse shifts attention from actions to identities. It suggests that danger resides not in what a person has done, but in what they think, read, or believe. This is a profound departure from traditional criminal law, which punishes conduct, not conscience.

For Muslim communities, this language lands within a pre-existing field of suspicion. Words like *radical* and *extremist* often function as coded references, understood socially even when not stated explicitly. When such terms enter official documents or media reports, they resonate far beyond the immediate case. They reinforce collective stereotypes, making neutrality difficult and empathy suspect.

Media amplification plays a decisive role here.

Television debates, newspaper headlines, and digital platforms repeat these terms with little interrogation. “Terror module busted.” “Sleeper cell uncovered.” “Radicalized youth arrested.” The repetition normalizes the vocabulary and discourages critical engagement. Rarely are these terms unpacked. Rarely is their evidentiary basis questioned.

By the time a case reaches court, public opinion has already been shaped.

This has tangible consequences for the justice process. Judges, though trained to be impartial, do not operate in a vacuum. Bail decisions, remand orders, and procedural discretion can be subtly influenced by the perceived gravity of labels attached to the accused. Defense lawyers must first dismantle language before they can even address facts.

From an investigative perspective, reliance on such terminology can also degrade professional rigor. When words substitute for analysis, confirmation bias sets in. Investigators may unconsciously interpret ambiguous evidence to fit a pre-existing narrative. Leads that contradict the dominant frame are deprioritized. The language closes rather than opens inquiry.

There is also an international dimension. Many of these terms originate in global counter-terror discourse, particularly post–9/11 frameworks developed in Western security institutions. When imported wholesale into different legal and social contexts, they often lose precision. What was once an analytical category becomes an administrative shortcut.

This is not an argument against naming threats. It is an argument for precision and restraint.

Effective counter-terrorism requires language that clarifies rather than condemns. Descriptions should be grounded in verifiable acts, not speculative intentions. Associations should be demonstrated, not assumed. Ideology should be distinguished from criminal conspiracy.

Several reforms are possible and necessary.

First, investigative agencies must adopt standardized definitions with legal oversight. Terms like *module* or *cell* should only be used once specific criteria are met and documented. Internal guidelines should prohibit their use at preliminary stages where facts remain untested.

Second, media institutions must revisit ethical standards for terror reporting. Descriptive accuracy should take precedence over sensational phrasing. Labels that imply guilt should be avoided before conviction. Editors must recognize that language can function as punishment long before a sentence is pronounced.

Third, courts should exercise greater scrutiny over terminology in charge sheets and remand applications. Judges can demand clarity: What evidence supports this label? Is it analytical shorthand or a factual conclusion? Such questions reaffirm judicial independence.

Finally, public discourse must resist the seduction of simplified narratives. Democracies depend on the ability to hold complexity without panic. When fear-driven language dominates, constitutional values erode quietly but steadily.

The language of terror does not merely reflect security concerns—it actively shapes them. When words are sharpened into weapons, they wound not only the accused, but the legal principles meant to protect all citizens.

Reclaiming precision in language is not an academic exercise.

It is a safeguard against injustice.

4: When Prevention Becomes Punishment

Preventive detention and the presumption of guilt

Preventive detention occupies a precarious space in any constitutional democracy. It is justified as a necessary exception, a temporary suspension of ordinary legal standards in the face of extraordinary threats. Its stated purpose is not punishment, but prevention. Yet in practice, preventive detention often functions as punishment in all but name—imposed without trial, sustained without conviction, and endured without meaningful recourse.

The danger lies not only in the power itself, but in how easily it becomes normalized.

Across jurisdictions, preventive detention laws are framed as tools of last resort. They allow the state to detain individuals based on the anticipation of future harm rather than proof of past crime. The threshold is not guilt beyond reasonable doubt, but suspicion deemed "reasonable" by executive authorities. This shift—from adjudication to anticipation—marks a fundamental departure from classical criminal jurisprudence.

In theory, such laws are accompanied by safeguards. In reality, those safeguards often prove inadequate when fear dominates governance.

The presumption of innocence is one of the cornerstones of modern legal systems. It requires the state to prove its case before depriving an individual of liberty. Preventive detention reverses this logic. Liberty is taken first, justification follows later—if at all. The detainee is placed in the impossible position of disproving an allegation that may never be fully articulated.

This reversal is especially pronounced in terror-related cases.

Authorities frequently argue that conventional evidentiary standards are unsuitable for terrorism, where threats are covert and networks opaque. While this concern is not entirely unfounded, it has led to a dangerous elasticity in detention practices. Vague intelligence inputs, unverified tips, or associations interpreted as ideological alignment are treated as sufficient grounds for incarceration.

The result is a system where suspicion hardens into confinement.

Preventive detention laws often allow for extended custody without filing a formal charge. Judicial oversight exists, but it is frequently procedural rather than substantive. Courts are asked to assess whether the detention follows the law, not whether the underlying suspicion is credible. Confidential intelligence is cited but not disclosed. Detainees and their lawyers are expected to contest shadows.

This creates a structural imbalance. The state possesses information it refuses to share, while the accused bears the burden of silence imposed by secrecy. Due process becomes an abstract principle rather than a lived reality.

For Muslim communities, preventive detention has a particular resonance. In environments already shaped by profiling and bias, these laws amplify existing vulnerabilities. Detention is not experienced as an isolated legal event, but as confirmation of a broader social suspicion. Families, neighbors, and employers rarely distinguish between detention and conviction. The stigma attaches instantly.

Time itself becomes a weapon.

Even when detainees are eventually released—often without charges—the period spent in custody cannot be undone. Employment is lost, education interrupted, mental health strained. In many cases, years pass before courts acknowledge that no prosecutable evidence exists. By then, the damage is irreversible.

Preventive detention thus achieves what prosecution could not: incapacitation without accountability.

From the perspective of governance, such laws offer political convenience. They signal decisiveness. They allow authorities to claim action in the face of public fear. Unlike criminal trials, they do not require the slow, uncertain work of evidence-gathering and cross-examination. The metrics of success become arrests and detentions, not convictions.

This incentive structure matters.

When institutional rewards are aligned with preventive action rather than judicial outcomes, the risk of misuse increases. Officers are encouraged to err on the side of detention. Ambiguity is resolved in favor of incarceration. Over time, exceptional powers become routine tools.

International human rights frameworks have long warned against this drift. Instruments such as the International Covenant on Civil and Political Rights permit preventive detention only under strict conditions and for limited durations. They emphasize proportionality, necessity, and effective judicial review. Yet implementation at the domestic level often falls short of these standards.

One recurring problem is the absence of clear temporal limits. Detention orders are renewed repeatedly, sometimes with minimal new material. Each extension is justified by the same untested fears that prompted the initial arrest. What begins as a preventive measure evolves into indefinite confinement.

Another concern is the erosion of evidentiary discipline. When detention does not require proof beyond reasonable doubt, investigative rigor weakens. There is less urgency to corroborate intelligence, less incentive to separate credible threats from speculative ones. Preventive detention becomes a substitute for investigation rather than a complement to it.

This undermines security rather than strengthening it.

A system that detains broadly but convicts rarely risks losing public trust. Communities become reluctant to cooperate with law enforcement. Intelligence dries up. Alienation grows. The very conditions that extremist groups exploit—grievance, humiliation, exclusion—are inadvertently reinforced.

A more effective approach is possible.

First, preventive detention must be strictly time-bound. Short, non-renewable detention periods force investigative agencies to either produce evidence or release the individual. This restores balance between prevention and prosecution.

Second, judicial oversight must be substantive, not symbolic. Judges should have access to the full evidentiary basis of detention, including classified material, and the authority to question its credibility. Where secrecy is unavoidable, special advocates or closed-court procedures can protect both security and fairness.

Third, transparency mechanisms are essential. Aggregate data on preventive detentions—disaggregated by outcome—should be made public. How many detainees are eventually charged? How many acquitted? Patterns reveal more than isolated cases.

Fourth, compensation and rehabilitation must be available for those wrongfully detained. Accountability cannot end with release. Without acknowledgment of harm, trust cannot be rebuilt.

Finally, language matters. Preventive detention should not be framed as proof of danger or guilt. Public communication must emphasize its provisional nature. The difference between suspicion and conviction must be preserved in law and discourse alike.

Security and liberty are not opposing forces. When preventive detention respects constitutional limits, it can serve its intended purpose. When it exceeds them, it becomes indistinguishable from punishment—administered without trial, shielded from scrutiny, and borne disproportionately by the marginalized.

A democracy reveals its strength not in how it confronts enemies, but in how carefully it treats those it merely fears.

5: Media as the First Court

Trial by media before legal proceedings

In contemporary democracies, the media is often described as the fourth pillar of the state—a watchdog meant to scrutinize power, inform citizens, and strengthen accountability. Yet in terror-related cases, this role frequently mutates into something else entirely. Long before a charge sheet is filed or a courtroom convenes, the media becomes the first court of judgment, delivering verdicts in prime time.

This transformation is neither accidental nor benign.

The logic of modern news cycles rewards speed over verification, spectacle over restraint. Terror-related stories, especially those involving Muslim accused, carry an immediate emotional charge. They promise fear, outrage, and a clear moral binary. In this environment, the presumption of innocence struggles to survive even a few hours.

Names are broadcast. Faces are displayed. Labels are affixed.

The language used is rarely cautious. Terms like "mastermind," "key conspirator," or "terror module member" are deployed as descriptors rather than allegations. Headlines speak of "crackdowns" and "major breakthroughs" while investigations are still in their infancy. The accused are no longer individuals under inquiry; they become characters in a predetermined narrative.

This narrative is constructed through selective leaks.

Investigative agencies often share partial information with favored media outlets. These briefings are framed as exclusive insights, but they are rarely subjected to independent verification. Journalists, under pressure to deliver breaking news, reproduce official claims with minimal scrutiny. The result is a feedback loop in which suspicion is amplified into certainty.

Once broadcast, these impressions are difficult to reverse.

When courts eventually intervene—sometimes years later—to acquit the accused for lack of evidence, the correction receives a fraction of the attention. Acquittals are reported quietly, often buried in inner pages or reduced to short columns. The original allegations, however, linger in public memory.

Media trials thus create a form of irreversible punishment.

The consequences extend beyond reputational harm. Trial by media influences legal processes in subtle but significant ways. Judges and prosecutors, though formally insulated from public opinion, operate within the same social atmosphere. High-profile media narratives can create pressure to deny bail, prolong detention, or frame charges aggressively to avoid appearing "soft on terror."

Witnesses, too, are affected. Publicly labeled suspects face hostility, intimidation, and social isolation. Potential defense witnesses hesitate to come forward. The accused's family members are subjected to scrutiny and harassment, effectively widening the circle of punishment.

For Muslim communities, this dynamic compounds existing vulnerabilities.

Media portrayals often emphasize religious identity even when it is legally irrelevant. Terms like "Muslim youth," "Islamic radical," or references to religious practices are woven into crime reporting, reinforcing the idea that faith itself is suspect. The distinction between individual culpability and collective identity erodes.

This is not merely a problem of bias; it is a structural issue.

Media organizations operate within economic and political constraints. Sensational terror coverage drives ratings and advertising revenue. National security narratives align conveniently with dominant political discourses. In such a climate, restraint is costly, while amplification is rewarded.

Yet the damage is profound.

Trial by media undermines the fairness of the justice system. It converts allegations into assumed truths and transforms investigative hypotheses into public facts. It also weakens the media's own credibility. When early claims collapse under judicial scrutiny, public trust erodes—not only in law enforcement, but in journalism itself.

International human rights standards recognize this risk. The right to a fair trial includes protection against prejudicial publicity. Courts in several jurisdictions have acknowledged that media coverage can compromise judicial independence and the rights of the accused. However, enforcement remains inconsistent, and self-regulation within media houses is often inadequate.

A more responsible model is possible.

First, clear naming protocols must be adopted and enforced. Until formal charges are framed, individuals should not be identified by name or photograph, particularly in terror-related cases. This practice is already standard in several democratic societies and does not impede legitimate reporting.

Second, journalists must distinguish between claims and facts. Language matters. Words like "alleged," "under investigation," and "unverified" are not legal formalities; they are ethical safeguards. Their consistent use can preserve nuance in a polarized environment.

Third, editorial independence from investigative agencies must be strengthened. Exclusive access should not come at the cost of critical distance. Media outlets must develop internal standards for evaluating official leaks, especially when they cannot be independently corroborated.

Fourth, equal prominence must be given to legal outcomes. Acquittals, bail orders, and judicial criticisms of investigations should receive coverage comparable to arrests and accusations. Justice is a process, not a moment of spectacle.

Fifth, regulatory bodies and press councils need real enforcement powers. Ethical codes without consequences are symbolic at best. Accountability mechanisms must be transparent, fair, and effective.

Finally, media literacy among audiences is essential. Citizens must be equipped to question narratives, recognize framing techniques, and understand the difference between investigation and conviction. An informed public is the strongest check against sensationalism.

Media freedom is a cornerstone of democracy. But freedom without responsibility can inflict its own form of violence—slow, pervasive, and difficult to undo. When the media becomes the first court, it often delivers the harshest sentence: social condemnation without appeal.

In a system committed to justice, the press must illuminate the path to truth, not preempt it.

6: Fear as a Governance Tool

The political use of terror narratives

Fear has always been a powerful instrument in the exercise of power. Unlike persuasion, it does not require consensus; unlike law, it does not require proof. It operates at the level of instinct, compressing complex realities into simple threats and urgent responses. In the context of terrorism, fear becomes especially potent—capable of reshaping public priorities, suspending skepticism, and legitimizing extraordinary state action.

What makes terror narratives uniquely effective as tools of governance is their elasticity.

The threat of terrorism is often framed as omnipresent yet undefined. It has no fixed borders, no clear timelines, and no easily identifiable end. This ambiguity allows political actors to invoke it repeatedly, adapting the narrative to suit changing objectives. Policies that would otherwise provoke resistance—expanded surveillance, prolonged detention, restrictions on dissent—are justified as necessary responses to an ever-evolving danger.

In this framework, fear becomes a resource.

Political rhetoric frequently amplifies isolated incidents into symbols of civilizational threat. Acts of violence are framed not as crimes to be investigated, but as existential challenges requiring immediate, decisive action. Nuance is portrayed as weakness; caution as complicity. The space for democratic debate contracts under the weight of urgency.

This dynamic is not limited to authoritarian regimes. Democracies, too, are vulnerable to fear-driven governance.

Elections are a particularly fertile ground for terror narratives. Campaigns that promise security over rights, strength over due process and decisiveness over deliberation often gain traction in polarized environments. The "us versus them" framing simplifies complex social realities into electoral slogans. Minority communities, especially Muslims, are cast as ambiguous insiders—citizens whose loyalty must be constantly demonstrated.

The consequences are structural, not episodic.

Once fear-based policies are institutionalized, they tend to persist beyond the immediate context that justified them. Emergency laws become permanent statutes. Temporary measures acquire bureaucratic inertia. The exceptional becomes ordinary. Citizens adapt to reduced expectations of privacy and liberty, while the state grows accustomed to operating with diminished scrutiny.

Fear, once normalized, rarely recedes on its own.

The political utility of terror narratives also lies in their capacity to redirect public attention. Economic inequality, governance failures, and social unrest are reframed as secondary concerns. Security becomes the master issue against which all others are measured. Dissenting voices are marginalized, accused of undermining national unity or aiding adversaries.

This conflation of critique with disloyalty is particularly corrosive.

Journalists, academics, and civil society actors who question counter-terror policies risk being labeled as apologists or sympathizers. The boundaries of acceptable discourse narrow. Self-censorship increases. The marketplace of ideas—essential for democratic resilience—atrophies under pressure.

For Muslim populations, fear-based governance translates into a lived reality of conditional belonging. Identity becomes politicized. Everyday practices—religious expression, social associations, political activism—are viewed through a lens of suspicion. The line between security policy and social control blurs.

This is not an inevitable outcome.

Research consistently shows that inclusive governance and strong civil liberties contribute to long-term security. Communities that trust institutions are more likely to cooperate with law enforcement, share information, and resist radicalization. Conversely, policies that stigmatize and exclude tend to produce the very alienation they claim to prevent.

Fear, in this sense, is a short-term strategy with long-term costs.

International experience offers cautionary lessons. States that have relied heavily on terror narratives often struggle to roll back expanded powers once the immediate threat subsides. Oversight mechanisms weaken. Executive authority expands. The balance between security and liberty tilts permanently.

Yet alternatives exist.

First, political leadership must commit to evidence-based communication. Public statements on terrorism should be grounded in verified facts, not speculation or exaggeration. Leaders have a responsibility to contextualize threats, not inflate them.

Second, security policy must be insulated from electoral incentives. Independent oversight bodies—parliamentary committees, judicial review panels, ombuds institutions—should evaluate counter-terror measures for proportionality and effectiveness. Transparency reduces the space for fear-based manipulation.

Third, minority protections must be explicit. Laws and policies should be audited for discriminatory impact, with mechanisms to address bias in implementation. Security that depends on collective suspicion is neither just nor effective.

Fourth, civic education plays a crucial role. Citizens equipped to understand risk, probability, and rights are less susceptible to panic-driven narratives. Democratic resilience depends as much on public literacy as on institutional design.

Finally, dissent must be protected as a democratic asset, not treated as a security threat. Robust debate strengthens policy by exposing flaws and unintended consequences. Silencing critique weakens the state's capacity to adapt and learn.

Fear may mobilize quickly, but it governs poorly.

A society governed by fear accepts trade-offs without scrutiny and sacrifices principles without necessity. In contrast, a society governed by law insists that security measures earn their legitimacy through accountability, proportionality, and respect for human dignity.

Terrorism poses real challenges. Ignoring them is neither responsible nor humane. But confronting them through fear-driven governance risks eroding the very foundations that terrorism seeks to destabilize.

The strength of a democracy is measured not by how loudly it invokes security, but by how calmly it protects both safety and freedom—without turning fear into policy.

7: Intelligence Inputs

"Secret sources" and the crisis of accountability

Modern counter-terrorism rests heavily on intelligence. Unlike conventional policing, where evidence is meant to be visible, testable, and contested, intelligence operates in shadows. Its value lies in secrecy; its authority derives from the claim that disclosure itself would cause harm. This logic has produced a troubling paradox: intelligence inputs that are powerful enough to justify arrests, detention, and prosecution, yet too confidential to be meaningfully challenged.

In legal terms, this is an anomaly.

In democratic theory, it is a fault line.

Intelligence is not evidence in the classical sense. It is raw, often fragmentary information—intercepts, informant tips, pattern analyses, foreign inputs—intended to guide investigation, not replace it. Yet in terror-related cases, intelligence frequently becomes the foundation upon which liberty is curtailed, without ever being converted into verifiable proof.

The phrase "based on intelligence inputs" has become a legal incantation.

It appears in arrest justifications, bail denials, preventive detention orders, and even charge sheets. Courts are told that sources cannot be disclosed, methods cannot be revealed, and materials cannot be shared. Judges are asked to trust, not to test. Defense lawyers are expected to argue in the dark.

This creates an asymmetry that strikes at the heart of due process.

The accused is denied the opportunity to confront the basis of the accusation. Cross-examination becomes impossible. Errors, exaggerations, and malicious inputs remain insulated from scrutiny. What begins as confidentiality morphs into un-challengeability.

Historically, intelligence agencies were meant to operate upstream of the criminal justice system. Their role was to flag risks, not to determine guilt. Over time, however, the boundary between intelligence and investigation has blurred. Intelligence assessments increasingly shape not just surveillance priorities, but legal outcomes.

This shift has consequences.

Intelligence is probabilistic by nature. It deals in likelihoods, associations, and inferences. Criminal law, by contrast, demands specificity and proof. When intelligence logic seeps into legal reasoning, standards erode. Ambiguity is tolerated. Corroboration becomes optional. Context is flattened.

One of the most troubling aspects is the reliance on "secret sources."

These may include paid informers, coerced collaborators, foreign agencies, or technical surveillance whose reliability cannot be independently assessed. Informers may have incentives to exaggerate. Foreign intelligence may reflect different legal standards—or political agendas. Yet once classified, these inputs acquire an aura of unquestionable authority.

The problem is not secrecy per se, but the absence of accountability mechanisms proportionate to the power exercised.

Courts often accept intelligence claims at face value, citing institutional competence or national security. In many jurisdictions, judges are reluctant to probe intelligence agencies aggressively, fearing accusations of overreach or naivety. This judicial deference, while understandable, weakens the adversarial process.

The result is a system where liberty is curtailed on the basis of trust rather than proof.

Errors are not hypothetical. Documented cases across jurisdictions reveal intelligence failures—misidentification, faulty translations, outdated information, or deliberate misinformation. In several high-profile acquittals, courts have later noted that intelligence inputs were either unsubstantiated or contradicted by material evidence. Yet such findings rarely trigger systemic reform.

Secrecy protects not only sources, but mistakes.

For Muslim accused, the burden is compounded by profiling dynamics. Intelligence assessments are often shaped by identity markers—religious practices, travel patterns, social networks—that are treated as suspicious without contextual grounding. What appears as "behavioral indicators" in intelligence jargon may, in reality, be ordinary aspects of life.

Once recorded, these indicators take on a life of their own.

Databases rarely forget. Intelligence entries persist even after acquittal or case closure. Individuals cleared by courts continue to face surveillance, travel restrictions, and secondary scrutiny. There is no effective mechanism for purging or correcting flawed intelligence records.

This creates a parallel system of punishment beyond the reach of law.

From a governance perspective, unchallengeable intelligence undermines institutional credibility. When agencies operate without external review, they risk groupthink and confirmation bias. The absence of corrective feedback loops weakens analytical rigor. Over time, intelligence becomes less reliable, not more.

Security suffers alongside liberty.

International human rights jurisprudence recognizes the legitimacy of intelligence secrecy, but insists on counterbalancing safeguards. These include independent oversight bodies, special advocates with security clearance, in-camera judicial review, and periodic audits. Where such mechanisms exist and function robustly, the tension between secrecy and fairness can be managed.

Where they do not, abuse flourishes.

A 360-degree solution requires structural recalibration, not rhetorical reassurance.

First, intelligence must be clearly demarcated from evidence. Intelligence can trigger investigation, but legal action must rest on independently verifiable material. Courts should insist on this conversion, not waive it.

Second, judicial capacity must be strengthened. Judges handling terror cases should receive specialized training in intelligence assessment, enabling them to question sources, methodologies, and reliability without compromising security.

Third, closed-court procedures should include independent special advocates empowered to challenge intelligence claims on behalf of the accused. Secrecy should not mean unilateral narrative control.

Fourth, intelligence databases must be subject to periodic review and correction. Acquittals and case closures should trigger mandatory reassessment and deletion of adverse entries, barring exceptional justification.

Fifth, oversight bodies must be genuinely independent, adequately resourced, and publicly accountable. Their findings—at least in aggregate form—should inform legislative and public debate.

Finally, accountability must extend to consequences. Where intelligence inputs are found to be fabricated, grossly negligent, or malicious, there must be penalties. Secrecy cannot be a shield for misconduct.

The legitimacy of intelligence agencies depends not on invisibility, but on trust earned through restraint and accountability.

A democratic state does not weaken itself by questioning power exercised in its name. It weakens itself when it refuses to. Intelligence, when confidential but unchallengeable, becomes an instrument of arbitrary authority. When subject to principled oversight, it can serve its true purpose: protecting society without abandoning justice.

The choice between security and accountability is a false one. A system that demands both is not naïve—it is resilient.

8: Profiling by Geography & Identity

When Muslim neighborhoods are designated "high-risk zones"

Security policy does not operate in abstraction. It is mapped—onto streets, neighborhoods, and communities. When geography becomes a proxy for suspicion, entire localities are transformed from living spaces into zones of surveillance. In counter-terrorism frameworks, this often takes the form of labeling Muslim-majority neighborhoods as "high-risk areas," a designation that carries significant legal and social consequences.

This practice is rarely announced explicitly, yet its effects are visible and measurable.

Policing patterns shift. Patrol density increases. Stop-and-search operations become routine. Surveillance infrastructure—cameras, informants, data collection—expands disproportionately. Residents experience heightened scrutiny not because of individual behavior, but because of where they live and who they are perceived to be.

Geography, in this context, becomes destiny.

The rationale offered is typically statistical or intelligence-based. Authorities cite past incidents, demographic concentration, or "radicalization vulnerability." However, such reasoning often conflates correlation with causation. The presence of a few suspects or incidents is extrapolated into a generalized risk profile for an entire community.

This leap is analytically flawed and legally problematic.

Profiling by geography and identity shifts the focus from conduct to characteristics. It undermines the principle of individualized suspicion, replacing it with collective inference. In doing so, it lowers the threshold for intervention and normalizes intrusive practices that would be unacceptable elsewhere.

The impact on residents is profound.

Daily life in a "high-risk zone" is shaped by constant visibility. Young men are stopped repeatedly. Homes are visited for "verification." Community events attract surveillance. Ordinary activities—gathering at mosques, organizing study circles, running charities—are viewed through a security lens.

Trust erodes on both sides.

Residents come to see law enforcement not as protectors, but as monitors. Cooperation declines. Information that could aid genuine security efforts is withheld. Alienation deepens. Ironically, the very conditions that authorities claim to prevent—social isolation, resentment, disengagement—are exacerbated by the policy itself.

Profiling also produces data distortions.

Increased surveillance yields more "hits"—more stops, more questioning, more minor infractions recorded. These statistics are then cited as evidence that the area is indeed high-risk, justifying further scrutiny. This circular logic creates a self-fulfilling prophecy, where attention generates data, and data justifies attention.

The cycle is difficult to break.

For Muslim communities, the designation of neighborhoods as high-risk reinforces broader narratives of collective suspicion. It spatializes identity-based bias, turning homes into suspect spaces. Children grow up internalizing the idea that their environment is inherently dangerous or suspect. The psychological toll is cumulative.

Legal challenges to geographic profiling face structural obstacles.

Policies are often informal, embedded in operational guidelines rather than codified law. This makes them difficult to contest. Courts may require proof of discriminatory intent, which is hard to establish when authorities rely on ostensibly neutral criteria like "risk assessment" or "intelligence mapping."

Yet international human rights standards are clear: security measures must be necessary, proportionate, and non-discriminatory.

Targeting entire neighborhoods based on identity fails this test unless supported by narrowly tailored, evidence-based justification—and even then, it demands strict oversight.

Comparative studies offer instructive contrasts.

Cities that have invested in community-based policing, social services, and inclusive governance tend to experience better security outcomes than those relying on blanket surveillance. Where residents are treated as partners rather than suspects, intelligence quality improves. Where dignity is respected, cooperation follows.

A 360-degree approach requires rethinking both strategy and assumptions.

First, risk assessment must be behavior-based, not identity-based. Geography can inform resource allocation, but it cannot substitute for individualized suspicion. Operational guidelines should explicitly prohibit profiling by religion or ethnicity.

Second, transparency is essential. Communities have a right to know the criteria by which they are classified and the mechanisms for review or appeal. Secret designations breed mistrust.

Third, oversight bodies should audit policing patterns for disproportionality. Data on stops, searches, and surveillance should be publicly available, disaggregated by location and outcome. Accountability begins with visibility.

Fourth, investment in social infrastructure must accompany security measures. Education, employment, housing, and civic engagement are not peripheral to counter-terrorism; they are central to it. Treating neighborhoods as problems rather than partners undermines long-term stability.

Fifth, dialogue must replace suspicion. Structured engagement with community leaders, civil society, and residents can surface concerns, correct misconceptions, and build mutual confidence. Security is most effective when it is co-produced.

Finally, language matters. The term "high-risk zone" carries implicit judgments. Policymakers should be mindful of how labels shape perception and policy. Neutral, precise terminology reduces stigma and promotes clarity.

Profiling by geography and identity may offer the illusion of control, but it delivers insecurity in slow, corrosive ways. It fragments citizenship, entrenches bias, and weakens the social fabric that security ultimately depends on.

A state committed to both safety and equality must resist the temptation to govern through maps of suspicion. True security is not achieved by marking neighborhoods as threats, but by ensuring that every neighborhood is treated as a part of the polity—worthy of protection, trust, and dignity.

9: The Informer Trap

Paid or pressured informers and the manufacture of false links

Informers occupy a paradoxical position in counter-terrorism. They are presented as indispensable—insiders who can penetrate secrecy, decode intent, and expose hidden networks. At the same time, they operate at the margins of legality and accountability, driven by incentives that often distort truth rather than reveal it. When improperly regulated, the use of informers becomes less a tool of intelligence and more a trap—one that ensnares the innocent while rewarding fabrication.

The reliance on informers thrives in environments of fear and urgency.

Terror investigations demand results under intense political and public pressure. Informers offer speed. They provide names, associations, and narratives that appear to connect disparate individuals into coherent plots. These stories are difficult to verify quickly, and their apparent insider status lends them credibility.

Yet credibility is not accuracy.

Informers are rarely neutral observers. Many are motivated by financial reward, leniency in their own cases, or protection from unrelated charges. Others act under coercion—threatened with prosecution, deportation, or social exposure unless they cooperate. These pressures create powerful incentives to exaggerate, embellish, or invent information.

False links are the natural outcome.

A casual acquaintance becomes a co-conspirator. A shared workplace becomes a meeting ground. A religious discussion becomes ideological alignment. Informers learn quickly what investigators want to hear. Over time, their narratives conform to expected patterns—networks, modules, hierarchies—regardless of the underlying reality.

Once recorded, these narratives take on institutional weight.

Investigative files accumulate layers of informer input, each reinforcing the last. Confirmation bias sets in. Contradictory evidence is discounted. The original source of the information recedes from view, replaced by references to "multiple intelligence inputs" that are, in fact, variations of the same unverified claim.

The accused faces a near-impossible task.

Informer testimony is often shielded by confidentiality. Identities are concealed. Motives remain undisclosed. Defense counsel is denied the opportunity to cross-examine or challenge credibility. Courts are asked to accept summaries rather than scrutinize substance.

This undermines the adversarial process.

For Muslim communities, the informer trap is particularly damaging. Informers are frequently embedded within mosques, charities, or social networks, turning spaces of trust into sites of suspicion. Ordinary interactions become potential evidence. Community cohesion erodes as individuals fear surveillance from within.

The psychological toll is significant.

People begin to self-censor, withdraw from communal life, and avoid political or religious expression. The line between civic engagement and risk becomes blurred. This environment of internal suspicion fractures social bonds and deepens alienation.

Documented cases reveal the consequences.

Courts in multiple jurisdictions have later dismissed cases built primarily on informer testimony, citing lack of corroboration or evidence of inducement. In some instances, informers were found to have provided demonstrably false information to secure payment or leniency. Yet accountability for these failures is rare.

The institutional response is often defensive.

Agencies argue that informers are a necessary evil, that their imperfections are unavoidable in the fight against terrorism. While it is true that human intelligence carries inherent risks, accepting those risks without robust safeguards is a policy choice—not an inevitability.

A more balanced approach is both possible and necessary.

First, informer use must be governed by clear, transparent protocols. These should define permissible incentives, prohibit coercion, and require documentation of interactions. Informers should not be allowed to operate in legal grey zones.

Second, corroboration must be mandatory. No arrest, detention, or charge should rest primarily on informer input without independent verification. Intelligence should trigger investigation, not conclude it.

Third, judicial scrutiny must be strengthened. Judges should be informed of informer motives, benefits received, and prior reliability. Where identities cannot be disclosed, alternative mechanisms—such as in-camera hearings—should allow for meaningful assessment.

Fourth, data on informer use should be subject to oversight. Aggregate statistics on cases relying on informers, their outcomes, and rates of acquittal can reveal systemic issues without compromising security.

Fifth, communities must be protected from infiltration that undermines fundamental rights. Places of worship and civic organizations should not be treated as intelligence hunting grounds absent specific, credible evidence of wrongdoing.

Finally, consequences matter. When informer-driven cases collapse due to fabrication or misconduct, there must be accountability—for both the informer and the supervising officers. Without consequences, the incentive structure remains skewed toward abuse.

Informers can play a legitimate role in security operations. But when incentives outweigh truth, they become architects of injustice.

The informer trap does not merely ensnare individuals; it corrodes the integrity of the system itself.

A justice system worthy of trust cannot rely on voices it refuses to examine. True security is built not on manufactured links, but on verified facts, accountable processes, and the courage to distinguish intelligence from evidence.

10: Custodial Confessions & Coercion

Why confession is not proof

Confessions have long occupied a privileged place in criminal justice. They appear decisive, personal, and morally conclusive. In terror-related investigations, where physical evidence is often limited or complex, custodial confessions are frequently presented as the ultimate validation of an investigative narrative. Yet decades of legal precedent and psychological research converge on a clear conclusion: confession does not equal proof.

When obtained in custody, it often signifies vulnerability rather than guilt.

Custodial environments are inherently coercive. The imbalance of power between interrogator and detainee is structural, not incidental. Isolation, prolonged questioning, sleep deprivation, and the uncertainty of indefinite detention create conditions in which compliance becomes a rational survival strategy. Under such pressure, the line between voluntary admission and compelled statement blurs.

This reality is well documented.

Courts across jurisdictions have repeatedly warned against the overreliance on confessions. International human rights law recognizes that statements obtained under duress—physical or psychological—are inherently unreliable. Yet in practice, confessions continue to anchor prosecutions, particularly in terror cases where other evidence may be weak or circumstantial.

The reasons are institutional.

Confessions offer narrative closure. They simplify complex investigations into a coherent story. They reduce the burden of proof. They allow agencies to claim success. In systems where performance is measured by arrests and charge sheets rather than convictions, confessions become convenient substitutes for rigorous investigation.

Coercion is not always visible.

While physical torture has declined in many jurisdictions, psychological coercion persists in subtler forms. Threats against family members, promises of leniency, manipulation of religious or emotional vulnerabilities, and the strategic use of fear are common tactics. Detainees may be told that cooperation is the only path to safety, or that resistance will result in harsher consequences.

These techniques exploit human psychology.

Research in cognitive psychology demonstrates that individuals under extreme stress are prone to false confessions. They may internalize suggested narratives, especially when repeatedly asserted by authority figures. Memory becomes malleable. The desire to end suffering outweighs the commitment to truth.

The problem is compounded by legal frameworks that privilege confessions.

In some jurisdictions, special anti-terror laws relax evidentiary standards, allowing confessions made to police officers to be admissible—contrary to ordinary criminal procedure. Safeguards such as prompt legal counsel, medical examination, and audiovisual recording are weakened or bypassed in the name of urgency.

This creates a dangerous incentive structure.

Investigators may prioritize extracting confessions over gathering corroborative evidence. Once a confession is secured, alternative hypotheses are abandoned. The investigative process ossifies around the statement, even when inconsistencies emerge.

For Muslim accused, the stakes are particularly high.

Confessions are often framed as ideological admissions, reinforcing stereotypes of radicalization. Statements taken under duress are presented as windows into extremist intent, rather than as artifacts of coercive environments. The cultural and linguistic barriers many detainees face further increase vulnerability to misunderstanding and manipulation.

Judicial scrutiny is uneven.

While higher courts have set standards for evaluating the voluntariness of confessions, lower courts may lack the resources or inclination to enforce them rigorously. The burden of proving coercion often falls on the accused, who may lack access to legal representation or medical documentation during detention.

The result is a system that mistakes compliance for culpability.

Empirical data underscores the risk. In multiple cases of wrongful conviction later overturned, false confessions played a central role. These cases are not anomalies; they reveal systemic vulnerabilities that persist wherever confessions are treated as decisive.

A credible counter-terror framework must address this head-on.

First, confessions should never stand alone. No conviction should rest primarily on a custodial confession without substantial independent corroboration. This principle must be codified and enforced.

Second, custodial safeguards must be non-negotiable. Immediate access to legal counsel, medical examination, and family notification are not procedural luxuries; they are essential protections against abuse.

Third, all interrogations should be audio visually recorded in their entirety. Partial recordings or selective transcripts undermine accountability. Full recordings protect both the accused and the interrogator.

Fourth, judicial training is critical. Judges must be equipped to recognize psychological coercion, not just physical abuse. Voluntariness must be assessed in context, not assumed from formal compliance.

Fifth, statements obtained under special anti-terror provisions should be subject to heightened scrutiny, not relaxed standards. Exceptional powers demand exceptional safeguards.

Finally, accountability must extend beyond exclusion of evidence. Where coercion is established, there must be consequences for those responsible. Without deterrence, abusive practices persist.

Confessions can be valuable when freely given, informed, and corroborated. But when extracted under custodial pressure, they become unreliable instruments of truth and dangerous tools of injustice.

A justice system that equates confession with proof abandons its commitment to reasoned adjudication. In the fight against terrorism, as in all serious crime, the legitimacy of the outcome depends not on how quickly guilt is declared, but on how carefully it is established.

Security achieved through coercion is fragile. Justice grounded in evidence endures.

11: Linking Unrelated Accused into One 'Module'

How Network Theory Is Misapplied to Manufacture Terror Cells

Introduction: When Analysis Becomes Architecture

In contemporary counterterrorism and national security prosecutions, a subtle but powerful transformation has taken place. Investigative analysis—originally intended to *describe* reality—has increasingly been used to *construct* it. At the center of this transformation lies the misapplication of network theory: a legitimate analytical framework repurposed to link otherwise unrelated individuals into a single, ominous-sounding "module," "cell," or "network."

This chapter examines how that process works, why it is so persuasive to courts and the public, and how it erodes fundamental principles of criminal law and human rights. Drawing on investigative journalism, legal analysis, and human rights research, it dissects the mechanics of network-based aggregation and proposes concrete safeguards to prevent analytical overreach.

The issue is not whether networks exist—they do. The issue is what happens when *the appearance of a network* is treated as evidence of criminal coordination, intent, or conspiracy, even when no such coordination exists.

I. Network Theory: From Descriptive Tool to Prosecutorial Shortcut

Network theory emerged as a way to understand complex systems—social movements, epidemiology, financial flows, communication patterns. In its proper use, it is probabilistic, contextual, and explicitly limited. It identifies *relationships*, not culpability.

In counterterrorism investigations, however, network theory is often stripped of its cautionary scaffolding. Analysts begin with a known or suspected individual and map outward: contacts, shared spaces, ideological overlaps, digital traces. What begins as exploratory analysis gradually hardens into an evidentiary claim.

The shift is subtle but decisive:

- **From correlation to coordination**
- **From association to allegiance**
- **From proximity to participation**

Once this shift occurs, the analytical map becomes a prosecutorial blueprint.

II. The Concept of the "Module": A Fiction of Coherence

The term "module" sounds technical, neutral, and scientific. In practice, it is often a narrative device—a way to group individuals who do not meet the legal threshold for conspiracy or joint criminal enterprise.

A typical "module" may include:

- Individuals who never met
- Individuals with no shared operational planning
- Individuals connected only through intermediaries or digital platforms
- Individuals separated by geography, language, or time

What binds them is not action, but *interpretation*.

The Elasticity of the Module

Modules are elastic by design. Their boundaries expand or contract depending on investigative needs. New names are added through tenuous links; inconvenient facts are framed as compartmentalization or operational security.

This elasticity makes modules difficult to falsify. Any absence of evidence becomes evidence of concealment.

III. Techniques of Artificial Linkage

Investigative records across jurisdictions reveal a recurring set of techniques used to link unrelated accused into a single module.

1. Shared Ideological References

Reading the same texts, following the same online preachers, or expressing similar grievances is framed as ideological coordination. This ignores the reality that mass ideologies—religious, political, or otherwise—are by definition shared by large populations.

Belief is transformed into behavior.

2. Digital Proximity

Algorithms privilege connection. Being in the same encrypted chat platform, forum, or social media ecosystem is treated as meaningful association, even when there is no direct communication.

Digital architecture becomes circumstantial evidence.

3. Geographic Coincidence

Living in the same city, passing through the same transit hubs, or attending the same public events is reframed as operational overlap. Urban density is mistaken for design.

4. Intermediary Contamination

One individual's proven wrongdoing is used as a contaminant. Anyone who interacted with them—even peripherally—becomes suspect. Guilt spreads not by evidence, but by adjacency.

5. Retrospective Narrative Assembly

Links are assembled *after* arrests, not before. Once individuals are detained, investigators search backward for connecting threads, weaving a story that did not guide the investigation but is presented as its foundation.

IV. Why Courts Are Vulnerable to Network Narratives

Network-based prosecutions succeed not because they are rigorous, but because they exploit structural weaknesses in legal systems.

Complexity as Authority

Judges and juries are often reluctant to challenge technical-sounding analyses. Network diagrams, metadata charts, and expert testimony create an aura of objectivity.

Complexity substitutes for proof.

The Fear Asymmetry

In terrorism cases, the perceived cost of under reaction dwarfs the perceived cost of overreach. This asymmetry biases decision-makers toward inclusion rather than exclusion.

Evidentiary Dilution

When multiple defendants are tried together, weak evidence against one is masked by stronger evidence against another. The module absorbs individual deficiencies.

V. Legal Consequences: The Collapse of Individualized Guilt

At the heart of criminal justice lies a simple principle: *liability is personal*. Module-based prosecutions erode this principle in three ways.

1. Intent Is Inferred, Not Proven

Rather than demonstrating individual reaction, intent is imputed from the alleged goals of the module.

2. Acts Are Substituted by Associations

Concrete actions give way to inferred roles: supporter, facilitator, sympathizer. These categories are often undefined and unfalsifiable.

3. Defense Becomes Fragmented

Each accused must simultaneously defend themselves and disprove the existence of the module itself—a near-impossible task.

VI. Human Rights Implications

The misuse of network theory has consequences far beyond individual cases.

Presumption of Innocence

When association becomes incriminating, innocence must be *proven*, not presumed.

Freedom of Thought and Expression

Ideological similarity becomes dangerous. Speech is criminalized retroactively.

Collective Punishment by Proxy

Communities become suspect ecosystems. Surveillance expands, trust erodes, and lawful dissent is chilled.

VII. Investigative Journalism's Role: Deconstructing the Module

Investigative journalists have been among the few actors capable of puncturing modular narratives.

Successful investigations share common features:

- Reconstructing timelines to show lack of coordination
- Mapping what *did not* happen
- Interviewing intermediaries to contextualize interactions
- Exposing analytical assumptions buried in expert reports

By slowing the narrative down, journalists reintroduce friction into stories designed to move quickly.

VIII. Toward a 360-Degree, Solution-Oriented Framework

Critique without reform risks cynicism. Preventing the misuse of network theory requires systemic change.

1. Evidentiary Firewalls

Courts should require explicit separation between exploratory intelligence analysis and admissible evidence. Network maps should never substitute for proof of individual conduct.

2. Methodological Transparency

Analysts must disclose:

- Criteria for inclusion in a network
- Error rates and false positives
- Alternative explanations rejected

3. Judicial Education

Judges need training in probabilistic reasoning, network analysis limitations, and cognitive bias.

4. Right to Analytical Cross-Examination

Defendants must be allowed to challenge not just conclusions, but *methods*—including data selection and modeling choices.

5. Sunset Clauses for Network Labels

Designations such as "module" or "cell" should expire unless continuously justified by new, individualized evidence.

IX. Reclaiming Analysis from Narrative Power

Network theory is not the villain of this story. Its misuse is. When analytical tools are weaponized to simplify complexity into guilt, they cease to illuminate and begin to obscure.

The task for investigators, journalists, lawyers, and courts is the same: to resist the comfort of coherence where none exists. To insist that evidence remains stubbornly specific. And to remember that systems designed to protect society must not do so by dissolving the individual into a diagram.

The danger of the manufactured module is not merely wrongful conviction. It is the normalization of a logic in which being *connectable* is enough to be culpable.

That logic, once accepted, does not remain confined to terrorism cases. It spreads—quietly, efficiently—into the architecture of justice itself.

12: International Templates, Local Misuse

How Global Counter-Terror Models Are Transplanted Without Local Safeguards

Introduction: When Universality Becomes a Blind Spot

Over the past two decades, counter-terrorism has become one of the most globalized domains of governance. Legal definitions, investigative techniques, surveillance technologies, watchlists, and prosecutorial strategies now travel rapidly across borders, packaged as best practices, model laws, or capacity-building assistance. International organizations, donor states, and security alliances promote a shared architecture of counter-terrorism—designed to be interoperable, scalable, and efficient.

Yet this very universality has become a liability. When global counter-terror templates are applied without regard to local legal cultures, political contexts, or institutional safeguards, they often mutate into tools of abuse. What was designed as a narrow response to exceptional violence becomes, in local hands, a mechanism for routine control.

This chapter examines how international counter-terror frameworks are misused at the national and sub-national level, why such misuse persists, and how it corrodes rule-of-law systems while remaining insulated from accountability. It argues that the problem is not international cooperation per se, but the uncritical transplantation of models divorced from the conditions that made them defensible—if only marginally—where they originated.

I. The Rise of the Global Counter-Terror Template

Counter-terrorism did not always travel so easily. Prior to the early 2000s, national security laws were largely domestic artifacts, shaped by local histories of conflict, constitutional design, and judicial oversight. This changed dramatically after major transnational attacks, when urgency produced convergence.

The Architecture of Convergence

Global counter-terror templates now emerge from multiple sources:

- United Nations Security Council resolutions
- Financial Action Task Force (FATF) recommendations
- Regional security alliances and intelligence-sharing blocs
- Bilateral security assistance and training programs
- Transnational policing networks

These instruments encourage states to adopt similar definitions of terrorism, criminalize preparatory acts, expand surveillance powers, and streamline prosecution.

On paper, the logic is compelling: terrorism crosses borders, so law must do the same. In practice, convergence often occurs at the level of *power*, not *protection*.

II. What Gets Exported—and What Does Not

International counter-terror models rarely travel as complete systems. Instead, they are disassembled, selectively imported, and reassembled within local legal environments.

Exported Aggressively

- Broad and vague definitions of terrorism
- Preventive detention regimes
- Expanded surveillance authorities
- Asset freezing and financial controls
- Lowered evidentiary thresholds

Exported Weakly or Not at All

- Independent judicial oversight
- Robust exclusionary rules
- Strong data-protection regimes
- Functional public defender systems
- Remedies for wrongful designation or detention

The result is asymmetry: states acquire the *teeth* of counter-terror law without its *brakes.*

III. The Local Context Problem

No counter-terror model is context-free. Legal systems differ in ways that fundamentally shape how extraordinary powers operate.

Fragile Institutions

In jurisdictions where courts lack independence, prosecutorial discretion is unchecked, or oversight bodies are politically compromised, imported counter-terror powers magnify existing dysfunctions.

Majoritarian Politics

Where political legitimacy rests on majoritarian identity, counter-terror laws become tools for disciplining minorities. Global language provides cover; local prejudice provides direction.

Emergency as Permanence

In states with histories of emergency rule, global counter-terror laws normalize exceptionalism. Temporary measures become embedded in ordinary criminal law.

IV. The Mirage of Compliance

International actors often assess counter-terror performance through formal indicators: laws passed, institutions created, trainings completed. This creates a compliance theater.

A state may:

- Adopt model legislation verbatim
- Establish specialized terror courts
- Create financial intelligence units

While simultaneously:

- Using laws against political opponents
- Ignoring procedural safeguards
- Blocking judicial review in practice

The appearance of compliance shields abuse from external scrutiny.

V. Case Patterns: How Misuse Manifests

Across regions, similar patterns emerge when global templates meet local realities.

1. Terrorism as a Residual Category

Acts that fail to meet ordinary criminal thresholds are recoded as terrorism. The template provides elasticity; local authorities supply targets.

2. Preventive Policing by Profile

Risk-based models imported from abroad rely on data that does not exist locally. Profiling fills the gap, often along ethnic, religious, or political lines.

3. Financial Regulation as Social Control

Asset-freezing regimes intended to disrupt funding networks are used to paralyze NGOs, charities, and informal economies.

4. Transnational Validation Loops

Once a local designation is shared internationally, it gains legitimacy. Foreign recognition replaces domestic proof.

VI. The Role of International Actors

Global counter-terror misuse is often framed as a domestic failure. This obscures the role of international enablers.

Strategic Blindness

Donor states prioritize cooperation over compliance. Abuses are tolerated if intelligence continues to flow.

Legal Ambiguity

International bodies rarely clarify minimum safeguards, preferring flexibility. This ambiguity invites exploitation.

Accountability Gaps

There is no effective mechanism to sanction states that weaponize global counter-terror frameworks internally.

VII. Human Rights Impact: From Exceptional Power to Ordinary Harm

The cumulative effect of template misuse is structural, not incidental.

Erosion of Due Process

Emergency procedures become default. Detention precedes evidence; secrecy replaces transparency.

Chilling of Civil Society

Organizations working on minority rights, dissent, or humanitarian relief operate under constant threat of designation.

Normalization of Collective Suspicion

Entire communities are treated as risk environments rather than rights-bearing populations.

VIII. Investigative Journalism and the Work of Translation

Investigative journalists play a critical role in exposing how global models are locally distorted.

Their work often involves:

- Tracing legal language back to its international source
- Comparing promised safeguards with lived practice
- Following funding and training pipelines
- Documenting the gap between paper compliance and ground

reality

By translating abstract frameworks into human consequences, journalism restores accountability.

IX. Toward Safeguard-Centered Globalization

The solution is not to abandon international cooperation, but to redesign it.

1. Safeguards as Non-Negotiable Exports

Any global counter-terror template must bundle powers with enforceable safeguards, not aspirational ones.

2. Contextual Impact Assessments

Before adoption, states should be required to assess how new powers will operate within existing institutional weaknesses.

3. International Review Mechanisms

Global bodies must evaluate not just formal compliance, but outcomes—arrests, acquittals, dismissals, and remedies.

4. Sunset and Localization Clauses

Imported powers should expire unless reauthorized through domestic democratic processes.

5. Protection of Civic Space

Explicit exemptions must shield journalism, humanitarian work, and lawful dissent from counter-terror overreach.

X. Rebalancing Universality and Responsibility

Global counter-terrorism was built on the promise of collective security. That promise fails when universality becomes an excuse for unaccountable power.

Templates are not neutral. When they travel without safeguards, they carry not only techniques but assumptions—about trust in institutions, equality before law, and limits on executive power—that may not hold.

The task ahead is not merely technical. It is ethical and political: to insist that international cooperation does not mean internationalized abuse; that security assistance does not become a license for repression; and that global models are judged not by how widely they are adopted, but by how narrowly they are applied.

Until safeguards travel as reliably as suspicion, the global counter-terror project will remain structurally incomplete—and locally dangerous.

13: Poverty & Limited Legal Access

How Economic Inequality Determines Who Receives Justice

Introduction: When Rights Exist Only on Paper

In every legal system that claims adherence to the rule of law, access to competent legal representation is treated as foundational. Constitutions promise equality before the law; international covenants guarantee the right to counsel; courts routinely affirm that justice must not depend on wealth. Yet in practice, poverty remains one of the most decisive predictors of legal outcome.

For marginalized families, the criminal justice system is not merely intimidating—it is structurally inaccessible. Quality legal defense is expensive, time-intensive, and concentrated among those who can pay. For those who cannot, legal rights become abstract assurances rather than lived protections.

This chapter examines how poverty and limited legal access interact to produce systemic injustice, particularly in serious criminal and national security cases. It explores how economic disadvantage shapes investigations, prosecutions, and outcomes, and why formal guarantees of legal aid often fail to offset these disparities. Finally, it proposes concrete, structural reforms aimed at transforming access to justice from a charitable afterthought into a core institutional obligation.

I. The Economics of Legal Defense

Legal defense is not a uniform service. It is a layered market in which quality, specialization, and independence correlate strongly with cost.

The True Cost of Competent Defense

Effective representation requires:

- Time to investigate facts independently
- Access to forensic, financial, and technical experts
- Capacity to challenge procedural violations
- Familiarity with specialized statutes and courts
- Willingness to litigate aggressively and persistently

Each of these elements carries financial cost. In complex cases—particularly terrorism, organized crime, or state security matters—the cost escalates dramatically.

For marginalized families, this cost is prohibitive. Legal defense becomes a matter of survival rather than strategy.

II. Legal Aid: Promise and Reality

Most jurisdictions provide some form of legal aid or public defense. On paper, these systems are designed to equalize access. In reality, they are often overwhelmed, underfunded, and structurally constrained.

Chronic Under-Resourcing

Public defenders frequently carry caseloads that make meaningful representation impossible. Time per client is rationed; investigation is minimal; strategic litigation is rare.

Structural Dependence

In some systems, legal aid lawyers are paid by the same state that prosecutes their clients. This dependence creates subtle but powerful disincentives to challenge authority aggressively.

Lack of Specialization

Complex cases require specialized knowledge. Legal aid systems rarely provide the training or continuity necessary for lawyers to develop deep expertise in national security or financial crime law.

The result is a two-tier system: one for those who can afford resistance, and one for those who must endure procedure.

III. Poverty as a Multiplier of Vulnerability

Economic disadvantage does not merely limit access to lawyers; it amplifies every other vulnerability in the justice process.

Early-Stage Disadvantage

Marginalized suspects are more likely to be arrested without counsel present, to waive rights unknowingly, or to make statements under pressure. Early procedural errors are rarely reversible.

Inability to Post Bail

Pretrial detention disproportionately affects the poor. Detention, in turn, weakens defense preparation, pressures defendants to accept plea deals, and fractures family support systems.

Resource Asymmetry

Prosecutorial agencies have institutional budgets, investigative machinery, and expert access. Poor defendants face the state alone, often with a single overburdened lawyer.

IV. National Security and the Cost of Silence

In terrorism and national security cases, economic inequality becomes especially consequential.

Secrecy and Expertise

These cases involve classified evidence, special procedures, and technical legal standards. Challenging them requires time, expertise, and institutional backing—resources rarely available to poor defendants.

Prolonged Detention

Lengthy pretrial detention is common, imposing financial devastation on families and eroding the ability to mount a defense.

Stigmatization

Once labeled a security suspect, families face social isolation, employment loss, and surveillance. Legal defense becomes only one of many unaffordable necessities.

V. The Family Burden

Legal inequality does not end with the accused. It radiates outward.

Financial Collapse

Families sell property, exhaust savings, or incur unmanageable debt to fund legal representation. Even acquittal does not reverse this damage.

Emotional and Social Costs

Prolonged cases destabilize households, disrupt education, and entrench trauma. Children grow up associating law with fear rather than protection.

Gendered Impact

Women—often spouses or mothers—frequently become de facto legal managers, navigating hostile institutions without training or support.

VI. Why Courts Tolerate Inequality

Despite its visibility, legal inequality persists because it is normalized.

Formalism Over Reality

Courts focus on whether counsel was formally appointed, not whether representation was effective.

Outcome Bias

Convictions are interpreted as validation of process, obscuring the role of unequal defense capacity.

Fragmented Accountability

No single institution bears responsibility for ensuring defense parity. The system functions through diffusion of blame.

VII. Investigative Journalism: Making Inequality Visible

Investigative journalists have played a crucial role in documenting how poverty shapes legal outcomes.

Their work often includes:

- Comparing defense resources across cases
- Exposing conflicts of interest in legal aid systems
- Following money trails behind "elite" defense teams
- Centering the experiences of families navigating the system

By reframing inequality as structural rather than individual failure, journalism challenges narratives of meritocratic justice.

VIII. Toward Equal Access as a Structural Obligation

Addressing legal inequality requires moving beyond symbolic reform.

1. Defense Parity Funding

Public defense budgets should be indexed to prosecutorial spending, ensuring baseline parity.

2. Independent Legal Aid Authorities

Legal aid must be institutionally independent from executive control.

3. Specialization and Training

Dedicated units for complex cases should be established within public defense systems.

4. Early and Automatic Counsel

Access to competent counsel must begin at first contact with law enforcement.

5. Family Support Mechanisms

Legal aid should include social support for families affected by prolonged proceedings.

Justice cannot be a luxury good. When legal outcomes track economic status, the law ceases to function as a public institution and becomes a market commodity.

The question is not whether marginalized families receive *some* representation, but whether they receive representation capable of resisting state power. Anything less is procedural compliance without substantive fairness.

A system that tolerates poverty-driven injustice ultimately undermines its own legitimacy. Equal access to law is not a concession to the poor; it is a prerequisite for the rule of law itself.

Until legal defense is treated as essential infrastructure rather than discretionary welfare, the promise of justice will remain intact only for those who can afford it.

14: Lack of Awareness about Rights

How Silence or Ignorance Is Mistaken for Guilt

Introduction: When Not Knowing the Rules Becomes a Crime

Modern legal systems presume a legally literate citizen. Rights are articulated in constitutions, statutes, and court judgments, often with great sophistication. But the distance between formal rights and lived awareness is vast. For millions of people—particularly the poor, the marginalized, the uneducated, and the socially excluded—the law remains opaque, intimidating, and alien.

In this gap between rights on paper and rights in practice, silence is routinely misread as deception, confusion as evasion, and ignorance as culpability. Individuals who do not know when to speak, when to remain silent, or how to assert their rights are penalized not for what they have done, but for what they fail to do procedurally.

This chapter examines how lack of legal awareness distorts investigations and prosecutions, especially in serious criminal and national security cases. It shows how ignorance of rights is transformed into adverse inference, how procedural missteps harden into evidence, and how legal systems normalize this transformation while maintaining the fiction of voluntariness and consent. Finally, it proposes reforms aimed at shifting the burden of legal clarity back where it belongs: onto the state.

I. The Myth of the Informed Suspect

Legal doctrine often assumes that individuals understand their rights once those rights are formally communicated. A warning is given; a form is signed; consent is recorded. The system moves on.

This assumption collapses under scrutiny.

Language and Comprehension Barriers

Rights are frequently communicated in technical language, unfamiliar dialects, or official jargon. For many suspects, especially those with limited education or literacy, comprehension is superficial at best.

Psychological Stress

Arrest, interrogation, and detention are inherently coercive environments. Fear, fatigue, and shock impair understanding. Information delivered in these conditions cannot reasonably be equated with informed choice.

Cultural Deference to Authority

In many societies, questioning officials is culturally discouraged. Compliance is mistaken for consent; silence is interpreted as strategy rather than fear.

II. Silence as Suspicion

One of the most consequential distortions in criminal justice is the transformation of silence into suspicion.

The Inference Trap

Although many legal systems formally protect the right to remain silent, investigators and courts often treat silence as circumstantial evidence. A refusal to answer becomes "non-cooperation." Hesitation becomes inconsistency.

Asymmetrical Expectations

Those who speak too little are suspected of hiding something. Those who speak too much risk self-incrimination. Navigating this contradiction requires legal sophistication that most suspects do not possess.

Retrospective Interpretation

Statements—or the absence of them—are reinterpreted later in light of prosecution narratives. Silence that preceded any formal accusation is framed as anticipatory guilt.

III. Consent without Understanding

Many of the most damaging rights violations occur not through overt force, but through purported consent.

Searches and Seizures

Individuals routinely "consent" to searches without understanding that refusal is an option—or that consent waives future legal challenges.

Statements and Confessions

Waivers of counsel and confessions are often obtained through rapid-fire procedures that prioritize form over substance.

Digital Access

Passwords, devices, and online accounts are surrendered without awareness of scope or permanence. Digital consent becomes total exposure.

In each case, ignorance is treated as agreement.

IV. National Security Cases: Silence under Suspicion

In terrorism and national security investigations, lack of rights awareness carries heightened risk.

Secret Procedures

Special laws often restrict disclosure, limit access to counsel, or permit delayed notification. Suspects cannot assert rights they do not know exist.

Criminalization of Non-Cooperation

Failure to answer questions, provide information, or assist investigations is sometimes criminalized, collapsing the distinction between silence and obstruction.

Cultural and Linguistic Distance

Security cases frequently target individuals from communities already distant from legal institutions. Misunderstanding becomes systemic.

V. How Courts Legitimize Ignorance

Judicial systems play a central role in converting ignorance into legality.

Formal Compliance Standards

Courts often ask whether rights were *read*, not whether they were *understood*. A signed form becomes conclusive proof.

Deference to Official Testimony

Investigators' accounts of voluntariness are privileged over suspects' descriptions of confusion or fear.

Burden Reversal

Defendants must prove they did not understand their rights—a near-impossible task.

VI. The Social Profile of Rights Ignorance

Lack of awareness is not randomly distributed.

Education and Literacy

Lower educational attainment correlates strongly with procedural disadvantage.

Migration and Citizenship Status

Non-citizens often fear that asserting rights will worsen their situation.

Poverty and Isolation

Those with limited exposure to legal institutions lack informal knowledge networks that others rely on.

Ignorance is produced by inequality, not individual failure.

VII. Investigative Journalism: Exposing the Consent Fiction

Investigative journalists have repeatedly revealed how rights ignorance is exploited.

Common methods include:

- Analyzing interrogation footage and transcripts
- Comparing official warnings with actual comprehension
- Documenting patterns across cases rather than isolated incidents
- Centering first-person accounts of confusion and coercion

These investigations puncture the myth that silence and consent are freely chosen.

VIII. Toward Meaningful Rights Awareness

Ensuring rights awareness requires structural, not symbolic, reform.

1. Comprehension-Based Standards

Legal validity should depend on demonstrable understanding, not ritualistic warnings.

2. Mandatory Early Counsel

Access to a lawyer should precede any waiver of rights.

3. Simplified and Contextual Rights Communication

Rights must be explained in plain language, adapted to literacy levels and cultural context.

4. Recording and Independent Review

Interrogations and consent procedures should be fully recorded and subject to scrutiny.

5. Public Legal Education

Rights awareness must be treated as public infrastructure, not individual responsibility.

IX. Reclaiming Silence as a Right, Not a Signal

Silence is not evidence. Confusion is not deception. Ignorance is not guilt.

A legal system that treats lack of awareness as culpability shifts responsibility away from state power and onto those least equipped to bear it. Such a system may appear orderly, but it is fundamentally unjust.

The measure of a rights-respecting system is not how elegantly rights are written, but how effectively they are understood and exercised by the most vulnerable. Until silence is protected as a right rather than interrogated as a signal, justice will remain conditional on legal literacy.

In that condition, the law does not merely punish wrongdoing—it punishes not knowing how to survive it.

15: Fear of Police = Self-Incrimination

How Coercive Power Turns Survival Behavior into Evidence

Introduction: When Fear Speaks Louder Than Words

In theory, the modern criminal justice system recognizes fear as an irrelevant emotion. Statements must be voluntary. Confessions must be free of coercion. Rights exist to protect individuals from the intimidating power of the state. In practice, however, fear is everywhere—and it is rarely neutral.

For millions of people, especially those from marginalized communities, interaction with police is not a neutral civic encounter. It is an experience shaped by history, rumor, observation, and often direct harm. Fear of police does not merely silence individuals; it alters behavior. And that altered behavior—hesitation, nervousness, inconsistency, over-compliance, flight—is routinely treated as incriminating.

This chapter examines how fear of law enforcement is systematically reinterpreted as evidence of guilt. It shows how survival responses are reframed as consciousness of wrongdoing, how coercive environments distort speech and memory, and how legal systems tolerate this distortion while preserving the fiction of voluntariness. Finally, it offers a reform framework aimed at disentangling fear from culpability and restoring meaning to the concept of free choice.

I. Fear as a Rational Response, Not a Moral Failing

Fear of police is often described as irrational or suspicious. This framing ignores empirical reality.

Historical and Structural Roots

In many societies, policing has been historically associated with repression, discrimination, or political control. For racial, religious, ethnic, and political minorities, fear is not abstract—it is inherited and reinforced by lived experience.

Contemporary Reinforcement

Media reports, community narratives, and widely circulated videos of police violence shape expectations. Individuals learn not from legal theory, but from observable outcomes.

Fear, in this context, is not evasion. It is rational risk assessment.

II. The Behavioral Trap: How Fear Produces "Suspicious" Conduct

Under stress, human behavior changes in predictable ways. These changes are routinely misread by investigators.

Nervousness and Inconsistency

Fear affects memory retrieval and speech. Minor discrepancies emerge, not from deceit, but from anxiety. Investigators often treat these discrepancies as lies.

Over-Compliance

Some individuals attempt to appease authority by answering everything, guessing when unsure, or agreeing with suggestions. These responses later appear as admissions.

Withdrawal and Silence

Others shut down entirely. Silence, avoidance of eye contact, or minimal responses are interpreted as non-cooperation.

Flight and Avoidance

Avoiding police contact—sometimes even leaving an area—is framed as consciousness of guilt, despite well-documented reasons to fear arbitrary detention or harassment.

Fear creates behavior; behavior becomes evidence.

III. Interrogation Environments and the Illusion of Choice

Police questioning is rarely a neutral exchange.

Power Imbalance

Officers control space, time, and information. Even without physical force, the imbalance is absolute.

Psychological Pressure

Isolation, fatigue, repetition, and implied consequences amplify fear. The line between persuasion and coercion blurs.

The Voluntariness Fiction

Courts often ask whether explicit threats were made, ignoring the cumulative pressure of the setting itself. Fear that is ambient and structural is rendered legally invisible.

IV. National Security and Policing Under Suspicion

Fear becomes especially consequential in terrorism and national security contexts.

Militarized Policing

Raids, armed presence, and aggressive questioning create environments where fear is unavoidable. Statements obtained in such settings are later treated as calm, reasoned disclosures.

Criminalization of Behavior under Stress

Inconsistencies, incomplete answers, or attempts to minimize exposure are framed as indicators of radicalization or intent.

Community-Wide Fear

Entire communities learn that interaction with security agencies carries risk. Avoidance becomes collective self-defense—and collective suspicion.

V. How Courts Convert Fear into Guilt

Judicial doctrine plays a critical role in legitimizing this conversion.

Credibility Assessments

Judges and juries often equate calmness with honesty and anxiety with deception, despite psychological evidence to the contrary.

Deference to Police Interpretation

Officers' interpretations of behavior are treated as expert insight rather than subjective perception shaped by bias.

Narrow Definitions of Coercion

Legal standards focus on overt threats or violence, excluding fear rooted in past experience or structural inequality.

The result is a system that punishes those most aware of its dangers.

VI. Who Bears the Burden of Fear

Fear of police is unevenly distributed.

Racial and Religious Minorities

Profiling and disproportionate enforcement create anticipatory fear.

Migrants and Non-Citizens

Fear of detention, deportation, or statelessness shapes every interaction.

The Poor and Previously Criminalized

Past encounters teach that asserting rights can provoke retaliation.

Fear reflects exposure, not guilt.

VII. Investigative Journalism: Reconstructing the Fear Factor

Investigative journalists have been instrumental in exposing how fear shapes outcomes.

Their work often includes:

- Analyzing interrogation footage for power dynamics
- Contextualizing "suspicious" behavior with community history
- Consulting psychologists to explain stress responses
- Tracking patterns across cases rather than isolated incidents

By restoring context, journalism disrupts simplistic narratives of guilt.

VIII. Toward a Fear-Aware Justice System

Reform must begin with recognition.

1. Behavioral Evidence Safeguards

Courts should restrict the use of demeanor-based inferences and require scientific grounding for behavioral claims.

2. Expanded Coercion Standards

Legal definitions of coercion must include psychological pressure and structural fear.

3. Mandatory Recording and Transparency

All interrogations should be recorded in full, with context preserved.

4. Early and Effective Counsel

Lawyers reduce fear by rebalancing power. Access must be immediate.

5. Policing Reform and Community Trust

Reducing fear requires accountability, demilitarization, and genuine community engagement—not public relations.

IX. Reframing Fear as Evidence of Power, Not Guilt

Fear is a signal—but not of criminality. It is a signal of power imbalance, historical memory, and lived risk. When legal systems treat fear-driven behavior as incriminating, they collapse the distinction between wrongdoing and survival.

A justice system worthy of the name must ask not why a suspect was afraid, but why fear was reasonable. Until that question becomes central, self-incrimination will continue to occur not through confession, but through the ordinary human response to authority.

In such a system, the most dangerous thing is not what a person says—but what fear makes them do

16: Long Pre-Trial Detention

When Time Becomes the Punishment

Introduction: Acquitted After a Decade, but Never Restored

In legal theory, pre-trial detention is an exception. It exists to ensure appearance at trial, prevent interference with evidence, or mitigate demonstrable risk. It is not meant to punish, deter, or incapacitate. In practice, however, long pre-trial detention has become one of the most powerful—and least scrutinized—punitive tools in modern criminal justice systems.

Across jurisdictions, individuals accused of serious crimes, particularly under national security or special criminal statutes, routinely spend years in prison before any determination of guilt. When acquittals finally arrive—sometimes after a decade or more—they do so quietly, without apology, compensation, or restoration. Time has already done its work.

This chapter examines long pre-trial detention as a structural failure masquerading as procedural necessity. It explores how delay becomes punishment, how detention substitutes for conviction, and how legal systems normalize prolonged incarceration while maintaining the formal language of presumption of innocence. Drawing on legal analysis, human rights research, and investigative reporting, it argues that excessive pre-trial detention is not a malfunction of justice, but an alternative mode of it.

I. The Legal Fiction of Temporariness

Pre-trial detention is justified as temporary. Courts speak of "custody pending trial," "interim detention," and "preventive confinement."

These phrases suggest brevity and urgency. Reality tells a different story.

Endless Pendency

Cases involving multiple defendants, complex statutes, or special courts often move at glacial speed. Investigations are extended. Charges are amended. Trials are adjourned. Appeals over bail consume years.

Detention continues not because guilt has been proven, but because time has not yet expired.

Procedural Legality, Substantive Injustice

Each extension of detention may be legally authorized. Taken together, they produce incarceration without judgment. The law permits what justice would forbid.

II. Why Certain Cases Never Reach Trial

Long pre-trial detention is not evenly distributed. It clusters around specific types of cases.

National Security and Terrorism

Special statutes lower bail thresholds, reverse presumptions, and allow extended investigation periods. Trials are delayed by secrecy, classified evidence, and institutional caution.

Politically Sensitive Prosecutions

Where cases carry political risk, delay becomes a risk-management strategy. Detention neutralizes individuals without the exposure of trial.

Mass or "Network" Cases

When dozens of defendants are tried together, procedural complexity becomes self-justifying delay. Individual liberty is subordinated to collective process.

In each scenario, detention becomes the system's answer to uncertainty.

III. Bail Denial as a System, Not an Exception

Bail is often described as discretionary. In practice, it is increasingly illusory.

Presumption Against Release

In serious cases, courts begin from suspicion rather than innocence. Bail hearings become mini-trials in which defendants must disprove hypothetical future risks.

Risk Inflation

Speculative concerns—flight, reoffending, public order—are invoked without evidentiary grounding. Poverty, lack of roots, or community stigma are reframed as danger.

Procedural Catch-22

Courts deny bail because trials are pending, then delay trials because defendants are detained.

IV. Detention as Coercion

Long pre-trial detention exerts pressure long before verdict.

Plea and Confession Pressure

Years in custody create powerful incentives to confess, cooperate, or plead simply to escape uncertainty.

Defense Impairment

Detained defendants struggle to meet lawyers, review evidence, or participate meaningfully in their defense. The longer the detention, the weaker the defense.

Psychological Attrition

Extended incarceration produces despair, dependency, and resignation. Legal resistance erodes.

Time becomes an interrogator that never stops questioning.

V. The Family Sentence

Pre-trial detention punishes not only the accused.

Economic Destruction

Income disappears overnight. Legal fees accumulate. Assets are sold. Debt becomes permanent.

Social Stigma

Families are marked by accusation. Even acquittal rarely restores reputation.

Intergenerational Harm

Children grow up visiting prisons, absorbing instability as normality. The law leaves marks long after it leaves cells.

Detention creates secondary victims without legal standing.

VI. Acquittal without Remedy

When acquittal finally arrives, it often arrives alone.

No Accountability for Delay

Courts rarely acknowledge systemic failure. Delays are treated as unfortunate but unavoidable.

No Compensation for Lost Years

Many systems offer no meaningful remedy for wrongful pre-trial detention absent proof of bad faith.

Presumption of Residual Suspicion

Acquitted individuals remain socially suspect. The time spent in jail is silently treated as partial justification.

Justice ends but harm remains.

VII. How Courts Normalize Prolonged Detention

Judicial doctrine sustains this system.

Deference to Prosecution Timelines

Courts accept investigative delay as necessity rather than choice.

Fragmented Review

Each bail denial is reviewed in isolation. The cumulative impact of years in custody is ignored.

Formalism over Proportionality

As long as procedure is followed, duration becomes irrelevant.

Time disappears from legal analysis, even as it defines lived reality.

VIII. Investigative Journalism: Following the Years

Investigative journalists have been essential in documenting long pre-trial detention.

Their work often involves:

- Tracking timelines across entire cases
- Comparing detention length with eventual outcomes
- Interviewing families during and after incarceration
- Exposing how acquitted individuals vanish from public record

By restoring chronology, journalism reveals detention as punishment.

IX. Toward a Time-Bound Justice System

Reform requires re-centering time as a legal harm.

1. Statutory Detention Limits

Maximum pre-trial detention periods must be enforceable, not aspirational.

2. Burden Reversal over Time

The longer detention lasts, the higher the burden on the state to justify it.

3. Mandatory Speedy-Trial Enforcement

Delays attributable to the state must trigger release, not excuse.

4. Compensation and Restoration

Acquittal after prolonged detention must carry automatic remedies.

5. Individualized Bail Review

Mass and network cases must not erase personal liberty assessments.

X. Reclaiming Time from the State

Time is the one punishment the state cannot return. When years are taken without conviction, the injustice is irreversible.

A system that allows prolonged pre-trial detention while proclaiming innocence does not merely fail justice—it redefines it. Punishment is no longer what follows guilt; it is what precedes proof.

The true measure of a justice system is not how severely it can sentence the guilty, but how carefully it guards the time of the innocent. Until time itself is recognized as a protected right, pre-trial detention will remain the most efficient conviction the state ever secures.

17: Family & Social Destruction

When Acquittal Ends the Case but Not the Punishment

Introduction: Freedom without Return

An acquittal is supposed to be an ending. In legal doctrine, it restores innocence, repairs reputation, and closes the file. In lived reality, acquittal often marks the beginning of a different struggle—one waged by families against stigma, suspicion, and social erasure. The law may withdraw its accusation, but society rarely follows.

For families of the accused, particularly in cases involving terrorism, national security, or politically charged crimes, the damage inflicted during investigation and trial does not recede with a not-guilty verdict. Years of surveillance, media exposure, detention, and rumor leave durable marks. Children are known by association. Spouses are reduced to caretakers and petitioners. Parents age under accusation. Even after release, the shadow of suspicion lingers, shaping employment prospects, housing, marriage, and community belonging.

This chapter examines family and social destruction as a systematic but largely unacknowledged outcome of modern criminal justice. It argues that stigma is not an accidental by-product of prosecution, but a predictable extension of how contemporary systems investigate, publicize, and delay. Drawing on human rights research, investigative journalism, and legal analysis, it explores how families become secondary targets, why acquittal fails to heal, and what meaningful restoration would require.

I. The Family as an Unnamed Defendant

Criminal law insists on individual liability. Practice tells a different story.

Collateral Suspicion

From the moment an accusation becomes public, suspicion spreads outward. Families are questioned, monitored, and socially marked. Innocence is treated as contagious in reverse: proximity to the accused becomes risk.

Informal Sanctions

Employers terminate contracts. Landlords withdraw leases. Schools treat children as liabilities. None of these actions require proof; accusation alone suffices.

Gendered Burdens

Women—wives, mothers, sisters—often absorb the administrative and emotional labor of defense. They become intermediaries between hostile institutions and fragile households, while themselves falling under suspicion.

The family is punished without charge, without counsel, and without remedy.

II. Media, Narrative, and the Permanence of Accusation

Media exposure is one of the most enduring sources of post-acquittal harm.

The Asymmetry of Coverage

Arrests and raids are public spectacles. Acquittals are procedural footnotes. Headlines announce suspicion; silence greets exoneration.

Digital Permanence

Online archives preserve accusation indefinitely. Search results reproduce stigma long after courts have moved on. Acquittal does not outrank allegation.

Narrative Inertia

Once framed as dangerous, families struggle to be re-imagined as ordinary. The story has already been told.

Media does not merely report cases; it fixes social memory.

III. Community Exile and Social Death

Stigma operates most powerfully at the community level.

Ostracism and Withdrawal

Neighbors avoid contact. Invitations stop. Religious and social institutions distance themselves to avoid scrutiny.

The Logic of Self-Protection

Communities internalize risk. Association becomes dangerous. Exclusion is rationalized as prudence.

Intergenerational Effects

Children inherit reputational debt. Their prospects narrow before choices are made.

Sociologists describe this condition as social death: life continues, but belonging does not.

IV. Economic Aftermath: Poverty after Freedom

Acquittal rarely restores economic stability.

Employment Barriers

Background checks, informal vetting, and rumor block access to work. Employers fear reputational harm.

Asset Depletion

Years of legal defense exhaust savings and property. Release comes without resources.

Informal Blacklisting

Entire families become "high-risk." Economic exclusion persists without documentation.

Freedom arrives without livelihood.

V. Psychological and Health Consequences

The impact of prolonged accusation extends beyond material loss.

Chronic Trauma

Families experience anxiety, depression, and hyper vigilance. The threat may be gone, but the body does not know it.

Identity Damage

Years defined by defense erode self-concept. People learn to introduce themselves through apology or explanation.

Breakdown of Trust

Institutions meant to protect—police, courts, media—become sources of harm. Civic alienation follows.

These harms are cumulative and rarely treated.

VI. Why Acquittal Fails to Repair

Legal systems are poorly designed for restoration.

Binary Outcomes

Courts determine guilt or innocence, not harm or repair. Once a verdict is delivered, the system disengages.

Absence of State Acknowledgment

Acquittals often come without recognition of error, delay, or excess. Silence substitutes for accountability.

Burden on the Innocent

Those cleared must rebuild on their own, often while still defending their legitimacy.

Justice ends where recovery should begin.

VII. Investigative Journalism: Following the Aftermath

Investigative journalists have been among the few to document life after acquittal.

Their work frequently includes:

- Revisiting cases years later
- Interviewing families rather than defendants alone
- Tracking employment, education, and social reintegration

- Challenging official narratives of closure

By extending the timeline, journalism reveals the hidden sentence that follows exoneration.

VIII. Human Rights Frameworks and Their Limits

International human rights law recognizes the right to remedy, dignity, and family life. Application remains weak.

Narrow Conceptions of Redress

Compensation regimes, where they exist, focus on detention, not stigma or social harm.

Lack of Collective Remedies

Families rarely qualify as rights-holders in criminal cases, despite bearing predictable harm.

Enforcement Gaps

Even favorable rulings often lack implementation mechanisms.

Rights exist, but restoration does not.

IX. Toward Meaningful Social Restoration

Repair must be intentional.

1. Right to Public Exoneration

States should be required to publicize acquittals with the same intensity as arrests.

2. Record Clearing and Digital Repair

Mechanisms must address online stigma, including search de-indexing and archival context.

3. Family-Centered Remedies

Compensation, counseling, and reintegration support should extend to affected families.

4. Employment and Housing Protections

Anti-discrimination safeguards must cover acquitted individuals and their households.

5. Community Reintegration Programs

Restoration requires collective acknowledgment, not private endurance.

X. Beyond Innocence: Reclaiming Dignity

The deepest failure of post-acquittal justice is not legal, but moral. A system that can destroy families through accusation, delay, and spectacle—and then retreat behind a verdict—mistakes procedural closure for accountability.

In such systems, innocence is fragile. It must be performed, defended, and repeatedly asserted. Dignity becomes conditional.

A rights-respecting justice system would recognize that the true measure of fairness is not how efficiently it prosecutes, but how fully it restores those it has accused and failed to convict. Until families are repaired alongside verdicts, acquittal will remain a narrow legal victory overshadowed by enduring social loss.

The case may end. The punishment should not.

18: Social Stigma That Never Ends

The "Once Accused, Always Suspect" Phenomenon

Introduction: The Accusation That Outlives the Law

In theory, criminal justice systems operate on a simple moral sequence: accusation, adjudication, resolution. Guilt is punished; innocence is restored. In practice, accusation has acquired a life of its own—one that often outlasts trials, verdicts, and even acquittals. Once a person has been named as a suspect, particularly in serious criminal or national security cases, suspicion becomes adhesive. It attaches not only to individuals, but to families, communities, and futures.

This chapter examines social stigma as a permanent, extrajudicial punishment—one that persists irrespective of legal outcome. It explores how suspicion becomes socially self-sustaining, how institutions quietly reinforce it, and how legal systems disclaim responsibility for damage they reliably produce. Drawing on human rights research, investigative journalism, and legal analysis, it argues that stigma is no longer an accidental by-product of justice, but a parallel system of control—informal, durable, and largely unregulated.

I. From Legal Presumption to Social Presumption

The presumption of innocence is a legal principle. Social life operates on different rules.

Suspicion as Social Memory

Communities remember accusation more vividly than resolution. Arrests, raids, and allegations are public, dramatic, and emotionally charged. Acquittals are procedural, delayed, and understated. Memory selects spectacle over correction.

The Cognitive Shortcut

Social psychology explains why suspicion persists. Once a narrative of danger is introduced, contradictory information is discounted. Acquittal is reframed as technicality; innocence as uncertainty.

The Burden Shift

The accused is no longer presumed innocent. Instead, they are expected to prove harmlessness indefinitely.

This is not prejudice in the abstract—it is a predictable outcome of how accusation is staged and circulated.

II. The Role of the State in Sustaining Stigma

Although stigma appears social, state institutions play a decisive role in producing and preserving it.

Public Accusation, Private Exoneration

States announce arrests loudly and often prematurely. Exoneration, when it occurs, is treated as administrative closure rather than public correction.

Residual Surveillance

Even after acquittal, individuals may remain on watch lists, databases, or informal police records. The law releases them; the system does not.

Bureaucratic Suspicion

Licensing authorities, employers, and immigration officials rely on background systems that privilege accusation over outcome.

Stigma is thus quietly institutionalized.

III. Media, Algorithms, and the Permanence of Suspicion

Modern stigma is digitally fortified.

Algorithmic Memory

Search engines and social platforms amplify the most clicked content—usually the initial accusation. Acquittals generate less engagement and are buried.

Context Collapse

Headlines travel without nuance. A name becomes searchable shorthand for danger.

Irreversibility

Unlike gossip, digital stigma does not fade. It accumulates, replicates, and resurfaces indefinitely.

Technology ensures that suspicion never truly expires.

IV. Community Logic: Why Stigma Feels Rational

Stigma persists not because communities are cruel, but because they are risk-averse.

Associational Risk

In environments shaped by surveillance and profiling, association itself becomes dangerous. Avoidance is interpreted as self-protection.

Collective Liability

Communities learn that one person's accusation can attract scrutiny to many. Distance becomes a survival strategy.

Moral Delegation

By treating acquitted individuals as permanently suspect, communities delegate moral judgment to the state, avoiding responsibility for reintegration.

Stigma is thus normalized as prudence.

V. The Unequal Distribution of Permanent Suspicion

Not everyone bears stigma equally.

Identity and Visibility

Minorities, migrants, and politically marginalized groups are less likely to benefit from doubt. Accusation confirms existing stereotypes.

Class and Power

Those with social capital can rebrand, relocate, or litigate reputational harm. The poor cannot.

Geographic Fixity

In tightly knit or over-policed areas, escape from stigma is nearly impossible. Identity becomes static.

Permanent suspicion follows predictable social lines.

VI. Legal Silence and the Abdication of Responsibility

Courts rarely address stigma.

Verdicts Without Repair

Judgments resolve charges, not narratives. Courts do not order restoration of reputation or reintegration.

Doctrinal Evasion

Stigma is treated as social harm beyond legal scope. The system disclaims consequences it foreseeably causes.

The Accountability Gap

No institution is tasked with undoing reputational damage. Harm persists by default.

Justice ends where social injury begins.

VII. Investigative Journalism: Tracing the Life of Suspicion

Investigative journalists have exposed how stigma operates over time.

Their work often involves:

- Revisiting acquitted cases years later
- Documenting employment, housing, and social exclusion
- Mapping watch lists, databases, and informal blacklists
- Challenging official claims of closure

By extending inquiry beyond verdicts, journalism reveals stigma as systemic.

VIII. Human Rights Law and the Right to Reputation

International law recognizes dignity and reputation as protected interests, but enforcement is weak.

Narrow Remedies

Defamation law addresses false statements, not true accusations that later prove unfounded.

Procedural Blindness

Human rights mechanisms focus on detention and trial fairness, not post-verdict life.

Collective Harm Ignored

Families and communities affected by stigma lack standing.

Rights exist, but stigma remains legally orphaned.

IX. Toward the Right to Be Un-Suspected

Ending permanent stigma requires structural intervention.

1. Symmetry of Public Communication

States must publicize exoneration with the same force as accusation.

2. Automatic Record Purging

Acquittal should trigger deletion from watchlists, databases, and secondary screening systems.

3. Digital Contextualization Rights

Individuals should have enforceable rights to contextualize or de-index accusatory content.

4. Reintegration Guarantees

Employment, housing, and licensing protections must extend beyond verdicts.

5. Community-Level Restoration

Restoration requires public acknowledgment, not silent endurance.

X. Reimagining Justice Beyond Suspicion

A justice system that allows suspicion to survive innocence has failed in its most basic promise: that accusation is reversible. When stigma becomes permanent, innocence becomes theoretical.

The "once accused, always suspect" phenomenon is not merely a social injustice—it is a structural one. It allows the state to exercise power without finality, to mark individuals indefinitely without conviction, and to disclaim responsibility for the social consequences of its actions.

True justice would recognize that clearing a name is not an abstract legal act, but a social one. Until systems are designed to undo suspicion as deliberately as they create it, stigma will remain the longest sentence the law ever imposes.

The case may close. Suspicion should too.

19: Wrongful Arrests after Blasts

When First Narratives Become First Arrests—and Truth Arrives Later

Introduction: The Pattern No One Admits Is a Pattern

In the aftermath of bombings and mass-casualty attacks, time collapses. Political pressure intensifies, public fear escalates, and investigative agencies are expected to act immediately. In this compressed moment, narratives harden quickly—often before evidence does. Across multiple jurisdictions and over decades, one pattern has recurred with disturbing regularity: **members of Muslim communities are among the first arrested, charged, or publicly named, only for later investigations to revise, abandon, or contradict those conclusions.**

This chapter does not argue that wrongful arrests are unique to any one group, nor that terrorism investigations are simple or risk-free. It examines something narrower and more serious: how *structural bias, investigative shortcuts, and narrative pressure* converge after blasts to produce predictable errors—and how those errors disproportionately affect already surveilled communities.

Drawing on documented cases, court findings, investigative journalism, and human rights analysis, this chapter traces how early assumptions become arrests, how arrests become prolonged prosecutions, and how later corrections fail to undo the damage. It asks not only *why* these wrongful arrests occur, but *why the system continues to repeat them despite knowing their cost.*

I. The First 72 Hours: Where Errors Are Born

Post-blast investigations operate under extreme constraints.

Political and Public Pressure

Governments face immediate demands for reassurance. Arrests signal control. Delay is interpreted as incompetence.

Media Amplification

Speculation circulates faster than verification. Leaks, unnamed sources, and "preliminary leads" shape public belief.

Existing Suspect Pools

Investigators turn first to communities already mapped through surveillance, informant networks, and prior cases. Familiarity substitutes for probability.

The result is not neutral urgency—it is guided acceleration.

II. Why Muslims Are Disproportionately Targeted Early

The pattern is not accidental.

Historical Conditioning

Decades of counterterror frameworks have trained institutions to associate certain forms of violence with particular identities.

Data Feedback Loops

Past arrests—regardless of outcome—populate databases that guide future suspicion. Wrongful arrests thus generate future wrongful arrests.

Legal Exceptionalism

Special laws lower thresholds for arrest, detention, and evidentiary sufficiency in national security cases.

Suspicion becomes institutional memory.

III. From Detention to Narrative Lock-In

Once arrests are made, reversal becomes difficult.

Confessions Under Pressure

Extended interrogation, isolation, and fear produce statements later rejected by courts—but powerful in early stages.

Associational Logic

Proximity, religious practice, or prior contact with suspects is treated as evidentiary weight.

Case Expansion

Weak evidence is reinforced by volume—multiple accused, overlapping allegations, and broad conspiracies.

The case survives by accumulation, not proof.

IV. Later Investigations, Quiet Revisions

In many documented cases, subsequent findings contradict early arrests.

New Forensic Evidence

Explosives analysis, call records, or witness testimony points elsewhere.

Alternative Networks Identified

Different ideological or organizational links emerge, often after years.

Official Reframing

Earlier errors are rarely acknowledged as wrongful; they are described as "initial leads" or "evolving investigations."

Correction occurs without accountability.

V. Courts and the Collapse of the Early Case

Judicial findings often expose the fragility of initial arrests.

Discredited Confessions

Courts reject statements obtained without safeguards.

Evidentiary Vacuums

Judges note absence of direct links between accused and acts.

Narrative Overreach

Broad conspiracy theories fail under scrutiny.

Yet these findings arrive years after liberty has been lost.

VI. Human Cost Beyond the Accused

Wrongful arrests reverberate outward.

Families under Permanent Suspicion

Relatives face surveillance, stigma, and economic exclusion.

Community Criminalization

Entire neighborhoods are framed as suspect environments.

Trust Erosion

Cooperation with law enforcement declines—not from hostility, but from fear.

Security weakens as legitimacy erodes.

VII. Investigative Journalism as Counter-Record

Independent journalism has been central to documenting these patterns.

Key contributions include:

- Reconstructing timelines that separate allegation from proof
- Comparing early police claims with final judicial outcomes
- Exposing reliance on coerced testimony
- Centering voices erased by official narratives

Journalism restores chronology—and accountability.

VIII. Human Rights Law and Discriminatory Impact

International law prohibits discrimination and arbitrary detention, even during emergencies.

Formal Neutrality, Substantive Bias

Laws may be facially neutral while applied unevenly.

Weak Remedies

Courts rarely recognize discriminatory investigation as a standalone violation.

Burden of Proof

Affected communities must prove bias within opaque systems.
Structural discrimination remains legally elusive.

IX. Why the Pattern Persists

Despite repeated exposure, the cycle continues.

No Cost for Error

Wrongful arrests carry little institutional consequence.

Reward Structures

Early arrests bring political credit; later acquittals bring silence.

Narrative Convenience

Simplified stories are easier to manage than complex truths.
The system learns the wrong lesson.

X. Toward Evidence-First Investigations

Preventing wrongful arrests after blasts requires structural reform.

1. Arrest Threshold Reform

Detention must be evidence-driven, not narrative-driven.

2. Independent Early Review

Neutral judicial or forensic review before prolonged detention.

3. Anti-Bias Safeguards

Mandatory bias audits in national security investigations.

4. Transparency After Revision

Public acknowledgment when early arrests prove unfounded.

5. Community Repair

Restorative engagement following wrongful targeting.

Conclusion: Security without Scapegoats

Wrongful arrests after blasts are not simply investigative mistakes—they are failures of institutional design. When suspicion follows familiar paths rather than evidence, justice becomes predictable in the worst way.

Correcting these errors years later does not restore legitimacy. It confirms what affected communities already know: that innocence is often discovered only after damage is complete.

A security system that repeatedly arrests the wrong people is not merely unjust—it is ineffective. Evidence-based investigation is not a concession to rights; it is a requirement of truth.

Until institutions learn to resist narrative reflexes and confront their own patterns, the cycle will repeat—at great human cost, and with diminishing credibility.

20: Confession-Only Cases

When Courts Reject Coerced Confessions—and the Case Collapses

Introduction: The Most Efficient Evidence

Confession has long been called the "queen of proofs." It is efficient, narrative-ready, and institutionally convenient. A confession shortens investigations, validates arrests, and reassures the public that truth has been found. Yet modern courts, forensic science, and human rights law increasingly agree on a sobering reality: **confessions are among the most unreliable forms of evidence—especially when obtained in custodial settings under pressure**.

Across jurisdictions, a recurring pattern has emerged. Individuals are arrested on suspicion, interrogated intensively, and induced to confess. Years later—often after prolonged pre-trial detention—courts reject those confessions as coerced, uncorroborated, or legally inadmissible. When the confession falls, there is nothing left. The case collapses.

This chapter examines confession-only cases as a systemic failure, not a collection of bad apples. Drawing on judicial reasoning, investigative journalism, and human rights analysis, it explores why confessions remain central despite their unreliability, how coercion is normalized, and why courts frequently discover—too late—that confession was the case. It concludes with reforms aimed at moving criminal justice from confession-driven closure to evidence-driven truth.

I. The Architecture of a Confession-Only Case

Confession-only cases follow a recognizable structure.

Arrest First, Evidence Later

Investigations begin with suspicion rather than proof. The arrest creates the urgency to justify itself. Interrogation becomes the primary investigative tool.

Isolation and Pressure

Extended custodial questioning, sleep deprivation, denial of counsel, and psychological intimidation are framed as routine. Physical coercion may be denied, but pressure is omnipresent.

Narrative Production

Investigators supply details; suspects supply assent. The confession is shaped to fit the theory of the case.

Evidentiary Substitution

Once recorded, the confession substitutes for independent verification. Leads are closed rather than pursued.

The confession does not crown the investigation; it replaces it.

II. Why Confessions Persist Despite Known Risks

The persistence of confession-only cases is not ignorance—it is incentive.

Institutional Efficiency

Confessions resolve cases quickly. They conserve resources and deliver outcomes.

Cognitive Bias

Once a confession is obtained, confirmation bias intensifies. Contradictory evidence is discounted.

Cultural Inheritance

Legal cultures trained on adversarial narratives continue to treat confession as moral truth, not contested data.

Accountability Asymmetry

There is little penalty for relying on a confession that later collapses. The costs are borne by the accused.

Confession endures because it works—for institutions.

III. The Mechanics of Coercion without Bruises

Modern coercion often leaves no visible marks.

Psychological Compulsion

Threats of harsher charges, promises of leniency, or appeals to family pressure induce compliance.

Temporal Exhaustion

Interrogations stretch over days. Fatigue erodes resistance.

Legal Ambiguity

Access to counsel is delayed or made nominal. Waivers are formal, not informed.

Scripted Truth

Investigators correct, refine, and rehearse statements until they align with the case theory.

Coercion operates through process, not spectacle.

IV. Courts Confront the Confession

When cases finally reach judgment, courts increasingly scrutinize confessions.

Voluntariness Tests

Judges assess the conditions of interrogation: duration, access to counsel, medical state, and consistency.

Corroboration Requirements

Confessions unsupported by independent evidence are rejected.

Internal Inconsistencies

Statements that evolve to match investigative needs lose credibility.

Procedural Violations

Failures to record interrogations or produce contemporaneous documentation undermine admissibility.

In many judgments, courts note that **the confession was the only evidence from the start.**

V. When the Confession Falls—and Nothing Remains

The collapse is often sudden.

Evidentiary Vacuum

No forensic links. No credible witnesses. No material corroboration.

Prosecutorial Retreat

Arguments shift from proof to probability, from certainty to suspicion.

Acquittal Without Vindication

Courts acquit for lack of evidence, not affirming innocence so much as rejecting the process.

The years spent imprisoned do not enter the verdict.

VI. The Human Cost of Confession-Driven Justice

Confession-only cases impose distinctive harms.

Internalized Guilt

Some accused come to believe the narrative they were induced to repeat.

Family Fracture

Confessions are used to pressure relatives, extract cooperation, or justify surveillance.

Stigma Amplification

A confession—retracted or rejected—lingers socially even after acquittal.

Time Lost to Fiction

Lives are reorganized around a story courts later declare untrue.

The damage persists beyond the judgment.

VII. Investigative Journalism and the Unmaking of Confessions

Journalists have played a critical role in exposing confession-only cases. Their work often includes:

- Obtaining interrogation transcripts and videos
- Comparing confessions with forensic timelines
- Interviewing interrogators and defense counsel
- Tracing how details appeared first in police notes, then in confessions

By reconstructing process, journalism reveals how truth was manufactured.

VIII. Human Rights Law: Clear Standards, Weak Enforcement

International norms prohibit torture and require voluntariness and corroboration. Practice diverges.

Formal Prohibitions, Practical Loopholes

Bans on coercion coexist with permissive interrogation cultures.

Burden on the Accused

Proving coercion years later is nearly impossible.

Remedies Without Deterrence

Excluding a confession does not address years of detention that preceded exclusion.

Law recognizes the problem; systems absorb it.

IX. Why Courts Discover the Truth So Late

Delayed scrutiny is structural.

Bail Denial Based on Confession

Early reliance on confession justifies prolonged detention, postponing rigorous review.

Trial as First Real Test

Only at trial are confessions fully contested.

Deference to Investigation

Early judicial stages privilege police accounts over defense challenges.

Time becomes the cost of skepticism.

X. From Confession to Corroboration: Structural Reforms

Ending confession-only cases requires redesign.

1. Mandatory Recording of Interrogations

Complete audio-visual recording from first contact to release.

2. Early Evidentiary Hearings

Courts must test corroboration before prolonged detention.

3. Right to Counsel as Practice

Immediate, continuous access—not formal availability.

4. Independent Forensic Standards

Confessions must align with verifiable facts unknown to investigators at the time.

5. Consequences for Reliance without Proof

Institutional accountability when cases rest solely on rejected confessions.

Conclusion: Truth Is Not a Statement

Confession-only cases reveal a justice system tempted by certainty without proof. When courts finally reject coerced confessions, they do more than acquit individuals—they expose a method that confuses compliance with truth.

The lesson is not that confessions should be ignored, but that **they must never be sufficient**. Truth in criminal justice is not spoken into existence under pressure; it is demonstrated through evidence that survives scrutiny.

Until systems abandon confession as a shortcut to closure and commit to corroboration as a standard of legitimacy, courts will continue to do belated cleanup—rejecting confessions years too late, after the damage has already been done.

Justice should not depend on who breaks first.

21: Youth Targeted for Online Activity

When Digital Expression Is Recast as Terrorist Intent

Introduction: The Screenshot as Evidence

In contemporary criminal investigations, particularly those invoking national security or counter-terrorism, the most decisive evidence is increasingly digital. Screenshots of messages, fragments of social media posts, browsing histories, and membership in online groups are elevated from context-bound expression to proof of intent. For young people—whose political curiosity, irony, experimentation, and peer interaction unfold primarily online—this shift has proven uniquely dangerous.

Across jurisdictions, documented cases reveal a recurring pattern: **youth are arrested, detained, and prosecuted based largely or entirely on their online activity**, only for courts to later find that the content did not establish intent, preparation, or participation in violence. The damage, however, is already done. Education is interrupted. Families are stigmatized. Futures are rerouted.

This chapter examines how ordinary digital behavior by young people is misinterpreted as terrorism. Drawing on judicial findings, investigative journalism, and human rights analysis, it traces how online expression becomes criminalized, why youth are especially vulnerable, and how legal systems struggle to distinguish ideology, speech, and curiosity from criminal conspiracy. It concludes by proposing safeguards that protect security without converting the internet into a dragnet for suspicion.

I. Youth, the Internet, and the Expansion of Suspicion

Young people live online not as an extension of offline life, but as its primary terrain.

Digital Native, Legal Orphan

Legal doctrines governing intent, conspiracy, and preparation evolved in an analog era. Applied to digital life, they flatten nuance and exaggerate risk.

Curiosity as Data

Following accounts, joining groups, or searching controversial topics produces a data trail that investigators may later reinterpret as trajectory.

Expression without Audience Control

Messages intended for peers, humor, or provocation are extracted from context and presented as fixed meaning.

The internet does not forget—and the law often does not contextualize.

II. How Online Activity Becomes a Terror Case

The transformation from post to prosecution follows a familiar sequence.

Platform Monitoring and Tips

Automated systems, informants, or peer reports flag content for review. Thresholds are opaque.

Selective Compilation

Investigators assemble a narrative by selecting alarming fragments while discarding mundane context.

Semantic Inflation

Metaphor becomes menace. Ideological discussion becomes endorsement. Anger becomes intent.

Absence of Offline Acts

In many cases, there is no evidence of planning, resources, or operational steps—only speech.

The case rests on interpretation, not action.

III. Why Youth Are Disproportionately Affected

Age is not incidental—it is central.

Developmental Vulnerability

Adolescents and young adults experiment with identity and belief. The law reads experimentation as commitment.

Digital Fluency, Legal Naïveté

Young people understand platforms better than procedures. They underestimate the permanence and reach of their speech.

Power Asymmetry

Interrogations exploit youth insecurity, fear, and desire to please authority.

Youthful behavior becomes retroactively criminal.

IV. Ideology, Speech, and the Slippage of Law

Courts are increasingly asked to police boundaries they were never designed to patrol.

Thought versus Action

Most legal systems reject punishment for belief alone. Online cases blur that line.

The Conspiracy Stretch

Loose online associations are recast as organizational membership.

Preparatory Elasticity

Reading, watching, or sharing material is treated as rehearsal rather than curiosity.

This slippage expands criminal liability beyond conduct.

V. Courts Push Back—Often Too Late

Judicial scrutiny frequently dismantles these cases.

Courts find no evidence of intent to commit violence.

Absence of Overt Acts

Online speech is not matched by real-world preparation.

Contextual Restoration

Judges note sarcasm, immaturity, or peer performance ignored by investigators.

Acquittals arrive after years of disruption.

VI. The Human Cost of Digital Criminalization

The impact on youth is disproportionate and enduring.

Educational Rupture

Detention and stigma derail schooling and careers.

Psychological Harm

Surveillance and prosecution during formative years produce lasting trauma.

Family and Community Fallout

Families absorb stigma; communities internalize fear of expression.

Punishment precedes proof.

VII. Investigative Journalism: Reconstructing Context

Journalists have played a key role in exposing misinterpretation of online activity.

Their investigations often involve:

- Recovering full message threads and timelines
- Interviewing peers to establish tone and context
- Comparing online expression with offline behavior
- Contrasting police narratives with judicial findings

By restoring context, journalism restores meaning.

VIII. Human Rights Law and Digital Expression

International standards protect freedom of expression, especially for youth. Practice lags.

Overbroad Restrictions

Security laws often criminalize vague categories of online conduct.

Chilling Effects

Youth self-censor political or religious discussion.

Weak Remedies

Even when acquitted, digital traces persist.

Rights exist; enforcement is uneven.

IX. Why the Pattern Persists

Despite repeated judicial correction, cases continue.

Technological Overconfidence

Data volume is mistaken for evidentiary strength.

Narrative Simplicity

Online posts offer ready-made stories of radicalization.

Low Institutional Cost

Few consequences follow collapsed cases.

Suspicion remains easier than restraint.

X. Safeguards for a Digital Generation

Security and rights are not opposites.

1. Contextual Evidence Standards

Online material must be evaluated in full context, including age and audience.

2. Action Thresholds

Speech alone should never suffice for prolonged detention.

3. Youth-Specific Protections

Mandatory counsel, parental notification, and developmental assessments.

4. Independent Digital Review

Experts should assess whether content plausibly indicates operational intent.

5. Post-Acquittal Digital Repair

Mechanisms to remove or contextualize stigmatizing records.

Conclusion: Protecting Security without Criminalizing Youth

Targeting young people for online activity reflects a system uneasy with digital culture and tempted by predictive policing. When curiosity is mistaken for conspiracy and expression for intent, the law abandons its most basic distinction: between thought and act.

Courts increasingly recognize this error—but recognition after years of detention is not justice. A system that treats youth expression as latent terrorism risks sacrificing an entire generation's trust for the illusion of foresight.

Security built on misinterpretation is fragile. Justice worthy of the digital age must learn to read online life not as prophecy, but as context—complex, provisional, and human.

Journalists play a crucial role in carrying judicial criticism beyond courtrooms.

They often:

- Translate dense judgments into public understanding
- Trace investigative failures across cases
- Question why similar lapses recur despite judicial warnings
- Hold institutions accountable for patterns courts identify

Journalism ensures that oversight does not remain buried in legal archives.

VII. Human Rights Law and the Duty to Investigate Properly

International human rights standards impose positive obligations on states.

Due Diligence Requirements

Investigations must be impartial, thorough, and evidence-based.

Remedy for Failure

Prolonged detention resulting from flawed investigations violates liberty rights.

Structural Accountability

Repeated lapses suggest systemic breach, not individual misconduct.

Yet enforcement mechanisms remain weak.

VIII. Oversight as Prevention, Not Autopsy

Transforming judicial oversight requires structural change.

1. Early Evidentiary Hearings

Courts must rigorously assess evidence before extended detention.

2. Continuous Case Management

Single-judge oversight to track delay and evidentiary development.

3. Disclosure Enforcement

Strict timelines and penalties for suppression of exculpatory material.

4. Written Reasons at Every Stage

Reasoned orders create accountability trails.

5. Data-Driven Review

Courts should track patterns of collapse and investigative failure.

Oversight must migrate upstream.

IX. The Institutional Resistance to Early Scrutiny

Reform faces resistance.

Fear of Overreach

Judges worry about encroaching on investigative autonomy.

Cultural Deference

Longstanding norms favor trust in police narratives.

Caseload Pressures

Time scarcity discourages deep early review.

These constraints are real—but not inevitable.

Conclusion: The Measure of Judicial Power

Judicial oversight matters most not when it eloquently dismantles a case after a decade, but when it quietly prevents one from becoming destructive in the first place. Courts that call out investigative lapses perform an essential democratic function—but their effectiveness is measured by timing as much as by courage.

A justice system that relies on late judicial intervention to correct investigative failure has already accepted years of unnecessary harm as collateral. True oversight would make such judgments rarer—not because courts are silent, but because flawed cases are stopped before they consume lives.

The strongest signal of judicial authority is not condemnation after acquittal. It is restraint exercised early, when liberty still has meaning.

22: Families Who Fought Back

Legal Resilience as a Survival Strategy

Introduction: When Defense Became Daily Life

In many of the cases examined so far, the criminal justice system appears as a grinding, impersonal force—slow to correct itself, resistant to accountability, and indifferent to collateral damage. Yet alongside this institutional inertia exists another, often overlooked story: that of families who refused to disappear. Faced with wrongful arrest, prolonged detention, social stigma, and economic exhaustion, some families transformed survival into strategy. They learned the law, navigated hostile bureaucracies, mobilized allies, and persisted for years against overwhelming odds.

This chapter examines **legal resilience**—not as heroism or exceptionalism, but as a necessity imposed by systemic failure. It documents how families became investigators, archivists, advocates, and informal legal workers when formal safeguards failed. Drawing on investigative journalism, court records, and human rights analysis, it explores the tactics families used to keep cases alive, the costs of sustained resistance, and the uncomfortable truth that justice often arrived only because someone outside the system refused to stop fighting.

I. From Shock to Strategy

The initial phase of a wrongful prosecution is typically marked by disorientation.

Arrest as Rupture

Raids, detentions, and public accusations fracture family life overnight. Legal language replaces ordinary speech. Fear displaces routine.

Learning Under Duress

Families are forced to acquire legal literacy rapidly—understanding remand orders, charge sheets, and procedural timelines with no preparation.

The Turn toward Strategy

When early hopes of swift correction fade, families begin to plan for endurance rather than resolution.

Resilience is not chosen; it is imposed.

II. Families as Parallel Legal Actors

Over time, families assume roles the system does not provide.

Case Archivists

They preserve documents, orders, transcripts, and correspondence—often more meticulously than institutions themselves.

Information Brokers

Families connect lawyers, journalists, activists, and researchers, maintaining continuity across years and personnel changes.

Procedural Watchdogs

They track missed deadlines, unexplained delays, and evidentiary gaps, pressing courts for movement.

These roles emerge because no one else fills them.

III. Economic Sacrifice as Legal Currency

Legal resilience is expensive.

Asset Liquidation

Homes, land, and savings are sold to finance defense.

Debt as Duration

Loans accumulate as cases stretch on, often long after acquittal.

Opportunity Costs

Careers are abandoned; education is deferred; health is neglected.

The price of persistence is often lifelong precarity.

IV. Gendered Labor of Resistance

Women disproportionately sustain legal resilience.

Administrative Burden

Wives and mothers manage paperwork, court appearances, and communication.

Emotional Containment

They absorb despair while maintaining family stability.

Public Interface

Women often become the visible face of advocacy, navigating stigma alongside responsibility.

This labor is essential—and largely invisible.

V. Engaging the Public Sphere

Some families move beyond courts.

Media Engagement

Strategic interaction with journalists reframes cases and counters official narratives.

Civil Society Alliances

Human rights groups provide expertise, legitimacy, and international attention.

Documentation as Defense

Families produce timelines, affidavits, and counter-records that later shape judicial understanding.

Public exposure becomes a protective mechanism.

VI. The Psychological Cost of Resistance

Resilience is not without damage.

Chronic Stress

Years of vigilance produce lasting anxiety and health problems.

Moral Injury

Families confront the erosion of faith in institutions meant to protect them.

Identity Reconfiguration

Life becomes organized around the case; selfhood narrows.

Resistance sustains survival—but at personal cost.

VII. When Persistence Changes Outcomes

In multiple documented cases, family persistence altered trajectories.

Correcting the Record

Inconsistencies surfaced because someone kept asking.

Preventing Erasure

Cases that might have quietly faded remained visible.

Enabling Judicial Courage

Well-documented defense records gave courts material to act upon.

Justice did not arrive spontaneously; it was pushed.

VIII. Investigative Journalism and Family Archives

Journalists often rely on family-maintained records.

Their reporting benefits from:

- longitudinal access to case materials
- firsthand accounts across years
- documentary evidence otherwise lost

Families become custodians of institutional memory.

IX. Human Rights Perspective: Resilience as Systemic Indictment

From a rights standpoint, family resilience reveals failure.

Inversion of Burden

Those harmed by the system shoulder the responsibility for correction.

Inequality of Outcome

Only families with minimal resources and stamina can persist.

Normalization of Endurance

Survival strategies risk becoming informal substitutes for reform.

Resilience should not be required for justice.

X. Supporting Families Without Romanticizing Struggle

Policy responses must acknowledge resilience without celebrating suffering.

1. Family Legal Support Units

State-funded assistance for families navigating prolonged cases.

2. Documentation and Disclosure Rights

Guaranteed access to records and timely information.

3. Economic Relief Mechanisms

Interim financial support during prolonged detention.

4. Mental Health Services

Trauma-informed counseling for families, not just defendants.

5. Institutional Accountability

Resilience should trigger reform, not replace it.

Conclusion: Courage in the Absence of Care

Families who fought back did so not because the system empowered them, but because it left them no alternative. Their persistence exposes both the fragility of justice and the strength of those forced to compensate for its absence.

Legal resilience should be understood not as a virtue demanded of citizens, but as evidence of institutional failure. When families must become lawyers, archivists, and advocates to secure basic fairness, the system has already abdicated part of its responsibility.

Their stories are not just accounts of survival. They are a mirror held up to justice itself—revealing what it requires from ordinary people when it does not work as promised.

23: Political Capital of Terror Fear

Elections, Security Narratives, and the Manufacture of Consent

Introduction: Fear as a Campaign Resource

In democratic theory, elections are moments of collective judgment—opportunities for citizens to assess governance, policy, and leadership. In practice, elections are also moments of vulnerability. Fear sharpens choices, compresses debate, and rewards certainty over nuance. Few fears are as politically potent as terrorism. It is immediate, visceral, and morally clarifying. It invites binaries: security versus chaos, loyalty versus threat, decisiveness versus doubt.

Across political systems, terror fear has become a form of political capital—accumulated, mobilized, and spent during electoral cycles. This chapter examines how the specter of terrorism is used to influence voters, reshape policy debate, and insulate state power from scrutiny. It does not claim that security threats are invented wholesale, nor that public fear is irrational. It asks a narrower, more difficult question: **how fear is operationalized once it exists, and how criminal justice systems become instruments in that process.**

Drawing on investigative reporting, electoral analysis, court findings, and human rights research, this chapter traces the pathways through which terror narratives migrate from crime scenes to campaign platforms, and from campaign platforms back into law enforcement priorities. It argues that when fear becomes electorally useful, due process becomes politically negotiable.

I. The Electoral Utility of Terror

Terrorism occupies a unique position in political imagination.

Moral Compression

Violence framed as terrorism collapses moral complexity. Causes, grievances, and context recede. What remains is the demand for order.

Authority Reinforcement

Strong executive action is rewarded. Calls for restraint are recast as weakness.

Agenda Displacement

Economic distress, corruption, and governance failures are sidelined by security urgency.

In electoral terms, terror fear is efficient. It simplifies choice.

II. Timing, Spectacle, and the Campaign Cycle

The political impact of terror fear is often shaped by timing.

Pre-Election Intensification

Security alerts, arrests, and raids frequently spike in the run-up to elections. Each action signals vigilance.

Media Synchronization

Round-the-clock coverage amplifies threat perception. Images repeat; analysis narrows.

Narrative Freezing

Early official statements harden into campaign talking points before investigation matures.

Even unresolved cases yield immediate political returns.

III. From Investigation to Messaging

Law enforcement activity does not remain confined to legal forums.

Selective Disclosure

Details emphasizing threat are publicized; evidentiary weaknesses remain confidential.

The Language of Prevention

Arrests are framed as having "averted" attacks, even when no operational planning is established.

Association as Proof

Ideological proximity substitutes for demonstrated action.

Investigations become raw material for political narrative.

IV. Voter Psychology and the Politics of Anxiety

Fear reshapes electoral behavior.

Risk Aversion

Voters favor continuity and authority when perceiving existential threat.

Out-Group Attribution

Blame consolidates around already marginalized communities.

Reduced Tolerance for Dissent

Civil liberties arguments lose traction; critique is equated with endangerment.

Terror fear narrows the democratic field.

V. Criminal Justice as Performance

Security policy increasingly performs reassurance rather than delivers accountability.

Arrests as Signals

Detentions communicate control regardless of evidentiary strength.

Prolonged Cases, Deferred Outcomes

Trials extend beyond election cycles. Political benefit is immediate; legal reckoning is delayed.

Quiet Acquittals

Exonerations, when they occur, rarely disrupt the narrative that already served its purpose.

Justice becomes temporally misaligned with politics.

VI. Investigative Journalism: Following the Political Trail

Journalists have traced how terror cases intersect with electoral strategy.

Their work often reveals:

- correlations between election calendars and security announcements
- discrepancies between early claims and later court findings
- political rhetoric built on cases that ultimately collapse
- institutional reluctance to revisit narratives after votes are cast

Journalism restores sequence—and motive.

VII. Human Rights Consequences of Electoral Security Politics

When fear dominates politics, rights are reframed as obstacles.

Normalization of Exceptional Laws

Emergency powers become permanent tools.

Discriminatory Impact

Targeted policing aligns with electoral majorities rather than evidence.

Chilling Democratic Participation

Affected communities withdraw from civic engagement.

The cost is borne unevenly, but democracy absorbs the damage.

VIII. Courts at the Edge of Politics

Judicial institutions operate within this charged environment.

Reluctance During Peaks

Courts are cautious when public anxiety is high.

Retrospective Correction

Judicial scrutiny intensifies after political urgency fades.

Limited Remedies

Courts address individual cases, not the political use of fear.

The separation between law and politics proves porous.

IX. Why the Strategy Persists

Despite exposure, fear-based politics endures.

Electoral Reward

Security posturing delivers votes.

Accountability Gap

Few consequences follow collapsed cases or exaggerated claims.

Narrative Asymmetry

Fear spreads faster than correction.

The incentives remain intact.

X. Safeguards against the Politicization of Terror

Reducing electoral misuse of terror fear requires institutional restraint.

1. Communication Protocols

Limits on pre-trial disclosure during election periods.

2. Independent Oversight

Non-partisan review of security actions proximate to elections.

3. Judicial Timelines

Expedited review of cases arising during campaign periods.

4. Media Standards

Contextual reporting obligations when cases are ongoing.

5. Post-Election Accountability

Mandatory review of high-profile security cases and outcomes.

Fear must not be electorally free.

Conclusion: Democracy Under the Shadow of Suspicion

The political capital of terror fear lies not only in its power to mobilize voters, but in its ability to suspend ordinary democratic judgment. When security narratives dominate elections, criminal justice becomes a stage, and citizens are asked to vote in a permanent state of emergency.

A democracy that cannot distinguish between vigilance and manipulation risks hollowing itself out from within. Terrorism demands serious, evidence-based response. But when fear becomes a campaign strategy, truth becomes optional and rights conditional.

The measure of democratic maturity is not whether leaders promise absolute security, but whether institutions can resist the temptation to convert fear into power. Until that resistance is built into electoral and legal systems alike, terror will remain not only a threat to life—but a tool of politics.

24: Institutional Incentives

Promotions, Funding, and the Pressure for "Quick Results"

Introduction: When Speed Becomes a Metric

Modern criminal justice systems rarely describe themselves as driven by incentives. Officially, investigations are guided by law, evidence, and public interest. Unofficially, however, institutions respond to metrics—clearance rates, conviction percentages, budget utilization, and career progression benchmarks. In security-related cases, especially those labeled as terrorism, these incentives become sharper and more consequential. Speed is rewarded. Visibility is valued. Outcomes are expected.

This chapter examines how **institutional incentives** shape investigative behavior, prosecutorial decision-making and inter-agency coordination. It does not assume bad faith or conspiracy. Instead, it traces how ordinary career pressures—promotions, postings, commendations, and funding—can distort priorities when combined with political urgency and public fear. The result is a system that quietly rewards early arrests and visible action, while under-valuing accuracy, restraint, and long-term accountability.

Drawing on investigative journalism, internal policy analysis, court observations, and human rights frameworks, this chapter explores how "quick results" become institutional currency—and how justice is compromised when speed substitutes for truth.

I. The Architecture of Incentives in Law Enforcement

Incentives are embedded, not announced.

Career Progression

Officers advance through a combination of seniority and performance assessments. High-profile cases carry disproportionate weight.

Performance Metrics

Clearance rates, arrests made, and charges filed are quantifiable; investigative integrity is not.

Commendations and Visibility

Public recognition often follows decisive action, not quiet correction.

These structures reward activity that can be counted.

II. Terror Cases as Career Accelerants

Security cases occupy a special institutional space.

Symbolic Value

Solving a terror case signals competence, loyalty, and resolve.

Organizational Prestige

Agencies compete for jurisdiction over high-profile investigations.

Fast-Track Recognition

Successful "operations" are linked to awards, media praise, and accelerated promotion.

The stakes extend beyond the case itself.

III. The Logic of Early Arrests

Under incentive pressure, investigations front-load outcomes.

Arrest as Proof of Progress

Detention demonstrates action, regardless of evidentiary maturity.

Narrative Lock-In

Once arrests are made, institutional credibility becomes tied to the prosecution's success.

Reduced Willingness to Revisit

Admitting error threatens careers and reputations.

Speed becomes self-reinforcing.

IV. Funding Cycles and Security Performance

Budgets follow perceived effectiveness.

Resource Allocation

Units that produce visible results justify continued or increased funding.

Grant and Central Assistance Models

Special security funds prioritize activity metrics over outcome quality.

Equipment and Training Incentives

Demonstrated threat levels unlock resources.

Financial structures mirror performance incentives.

V. Prosecutorial Alignment and Case Persistence

Incentives do not stop with police.

Conviction Statistics

Prosecutors are evaluated on success rates, not withdrawal of weak cases.

Institutional Solidarity

Challenging investigative flaws risks inter-agency friction.

Delay as Strategy

Prolonged trials defer accountability beyond individual tenures.

Weak cases acquire institutional momentum.

VI. Judicial Observations on Incentive Distortion

Courts occasionally acknowledge incentive-driven failure.

Judgments have noted:

- investigations driven by "haste" rather than rigor
- over-reliance on confession to meet timelines
- disregard for contradictory evidence
- mechanical filing of charges without independent evaluation

Such observations are rare—but revealing.

VII. Investigative Journalism: Following the Money and the Files

Journalists have uncovered patterns invisible in individual cases.

Their reporting highlights:

- correlation between promotions and high-profile arrests
- repeated investigative shortcuts by rewarded units

- funding renewals following publicized operations
- silence when cases later collapse

Incentives leave paper trails.

VIII. Human Rights Analysis: Structural Risk Factors

From a human rights perspective, incentive misalignment is a systemic risk.

Foreseeability of Harm

When speed is rewarded, rights violations are predictable.

Discriminatory Impact

Marginalized groups absorb the cost of institutional ambition.

State Responsibility

Governments are accountable not only for actions, but for incentive design.

Structural bias requires structural remedy.

IX. The Culture of Non-Correction

Perhaps the most damaging incentive is the absence of penalty for error.

No Cost for Collapse

Acquittals rarely trigger internal review.

Career Mobility

Officers move posts before cases conclude.

Institutional Amnesia

Failures are individualized and forgotten.

Without consequence, distortion persists.

X. Reimagining Incentives for Accuracy

Reform requires changing what institutions reward.

1. Accuracy-Based Evaluation

Performance metrics should include case durability, not just speed.

2. Credit for Withdrawal

Early recognition for identifying and closing weak cases.

3. Independent Review Boards

Career-impacting audits of collapsed prosecutions.

4. Funding Linked to Compliance

Budgets contingent on rights adherence and disclosure practices.

5. Transparent Career Histories

Public record of case outcomes linked to officials.

Incentives shape behavior. They must be redesigned.

XI. The Political Dimension of Institutional Reward

Incentives are reinforced by politics.

Alignment with Electoral Narratives

Security success stories serve political needs.

Protection from Scrutiny

Politically useful cases receive institutional shielding.

Shared Risk Avoidance

No actor wants to be the first to question a celebrated investigation.

Institutional and political incentives converge.

Conclusion: Measuring What Matters

The persistence of weak terror prosecutions cannot be understood solely as error or prejudice. It is also the product of incentive structures that reward visibility over verification, speed over substance, and arrest over accuracy.

Institutions do what they are rewarded to do. When promotions, funding, and prestige flow from "quick results," the system quietly encourages premature conclusions and resists correction. The damage—to individuals, communities, and democratic trust—is predictable and recurring.

A justice system serious about truth must measure success differently. It must reward those who slow down, question assumptions, disclose weaknesses, and correct course early. Until incentives align with accuracy and rights, investigative failure will not be an anomaly. It will be an outcome.

25: Media Ratings Economy

When Terror Sells: Sensationalism and the Shaping of Public Perception

Introduction: Fear as a Commodity

In contemporary societies, media is not merely an observer of events; it is a marketplace. Ratings, clicks, subscriptions, and advertising revenue incentivize content that captures attention quickly and emotionally. Few subjects capture attention as effectively as terrorism. Images of destruction, declarations of threat, and the drama of arrests are consumed eagerly, shared widely, and monetized efficiently.

This chapter examines how the media economy intersects with security narratives to shape public perception, influence policy, and indirectly affect criminal justice outcomes. It does not argue that journalists invent terrorism, nor that reporting is universally bad. Rather, it demonstrates how market pressures amplify sensationalism, compress context, and produce enduring effects on both society and institutions.

Drawing on media studies, investigative reporting, human rights research, and legal analysis, this chapter maps how terror sells, why sensational coverage is institutionally reinforced, and what reforms could preserve both commercial viability and civic integrity.

I. The Economics of News

Attention as Currency

Ratings, clicks, and shares are quantifiable. Coverage that triggers emotional engagement outperforms detailed, nuanced reporting.

Terrorism—a subject inherently dramatic—becomes a guaranteed attention driver.

The Feedback Loop

High engagement leads to repeated coverage, reinforcing both audience expectation and newsroom priorities. Media outlets learn that fear commands attention faster than investigation.

Competition for Visibility

Multiple outlets covering the same story escalate urgency, often privileging immediacy over accuracy.

The economic structure incentivizes speed, drama, and repetition.

II. Sensationalism and Its Forms

Headlines and Imagery

Bold, alarming titles and images of violence create immediate cognitive impact.

Selective Detail

Focus on arrests, threat, and worst-case scenarios while downplaying context or uncertainty.

Personalization and Villainization

Stories often center on individuals as embodiments of terror rather than on the broader circumstances.

Serial Coverage

Repeated updates, even minor, reinforce the narrative of imminent danger.

The cumulative effect is a heightened perception of risk.

III. Media Influence on Public Perception

Fear Amplification

Audience perception of threat exceeds statistical reality.

Moral Simplification

Complex socio-political factors are reduced to binary narratives: good vs. evil, us vs. them.

Behavioral Change

Public anxiety affects voting, consumption, and social interaction.

Sensationalism is not merely storytelling; it shapes social reality.

IV. The Interaction between Media and Justice

Early Framing of Investigations

Initial media reports often become reference points for later narratives, influencing both public opinion and institutional behavior.

Pre-Trial Contamination

Coverage may pressure law enforcement to prioritize visibility, contributing to the emphasis on quick arrests and high-profile cases.

Selective Memory

Once a narrative is embedded, acquittals and corrections receive far less attention.

Media becomes both a magnifier and a conveyor of institutional urgency.

V. Case Study Analysis

Investigative journalism and legal review show recurring patterns:

- arrests highlighted for public reassurance, later overturned
- digital messaging or social media posts framed as proof of intent in sensationalized reporting
- narrative persistence despite lack of evidence or judicial rejection

Patterns suggest systemic reinforcement between news cycles, investigative haste, and public perception.

VI. Market Pressures on Ethical Reporting

Time-to-Publish Imperative

Speed undermines context, verification, and balanced narrative.

Audience Metrics as Decision Driver

Content selection often follows algorithmic optimization rather than editorial deliberation.

Organizational Incentives

Recognition, awards, and circulation targets favor high-impact reporting over meticulous analysis.

Economic pressures shape journalistic priorities, often unconsciously.

VII. Human Rights Implications

Presumption of Guilt

Pre-trial coverage can stigmatize accused individuals, shaping social and legal perception before adjudication.

Community Profiling

Media narratives disproportionately affect marginalized groups, reinforcing societal bias.

Chilling Effect on Speech

Fear of misinterpretation or exposure inhibits legitimate expression.

The costs of sensationalism extend far beyond immediate consumption.

VIII. Journalistic Responsibility and Investigative Standards

Some media outlets demonstrate resistance to the ratings economy:

- rigorous verification before publication
- contextual reporting and historical framing
- foregrounding judicial outcomes and acquittals
- transparent correction mechanisms

These practices demonstrate that economic pressures can be mitigated, though not eliminated.

IX. Institutional Feedback Loops

Reinforcing Quick Arrests

Sensational reporting rewards immediate action by law enforcement, aligning media and institutional incentives.

Political Exploitation

High-profile coverage amplifies fear, benefiting political actors and reinforcing cycles of securitization.

Public Expectation

Audiences conditioned to expect drama pressure both media and institutions to perform, rather than deliberate.

Media ratings, politics, and investigative urgency form a mutually reinforcing loop.

X. Potential Reforms

Editorial Standards for Pre-Trial Coverage

Guidelines to balance public interest with presumption of innocence.

Transparency Mechanisms

Publish corrections, clarifications, and judicial outcomes prominently.

Audience Media Literacy

Education programs to contextualize news, particularly security-related reporting.

Incentive Restructuring

Recognition systems that reward accuracy, depth, and ethical reporting alongside engagement metrics.

Institutional Awareness

Law enforcement and judicial actors must recognize media pressure as an operational factor and resist hasty action.

Conclusion: Navigating the Ratings Economy

Terrorism coverage demonstrates the interplay of fear, economics, and perception. Media organizations are caught between the imperatives of audience engagement and civic responsibility. Law enforcement, political actors, and public perception are all influenced by the dynamics of visibility, drama, and speed.

Managing this ecosystem requires conscious intervention: from newsroom ethics and literacy programs to institutional protocols and incentive alignment. Without deliberate adjustment, fear will continue to be both consumed and produced, with profound consequences for justice, civil rights, and democratic deliberation.

26: Silence of the Majority

When Injustice Feels Distant, It Persists

Introduction: The Cost of Indifference

In a society marked by repeated instances of investigative shortcuts, wrongful arrests, and sensationalized terror narratives, there is a pervasive yet often invisible phenomenon: **the silence of the majority**. While a few families fight tirelessly, some journalists expose patterns, and certain judges intervene belatedly, the majority—citizens, civil society actors, and even political constituencies—remain largely unengaged. This lack of collective action does not indicate approval; it signals distance, distraction, and resignation. Yet the consequences are profound: injustice persists precisely because societal pressure is uneven, selective, and episodic.

This chapter examines the mechanisms and effects of societal silence, exploring why large populations tolerate systemic injustice at a remove, how media and politics reinforce passivity, and what strategies might transform quiet complicity into constructive engagement. Drawing on investigative reporting, human rights frameworks, and political sociology, it emphasizes that the endurance of flawed systems depends as much on collective inaction as on institutional design.

I. The Geography of Inattention

Psychological Distance

When wrongful detentions, coerced confessions, or procedural failures occur in marginalized communities, the majority experiences them as distant. Urban residents may ignore rural raids; politically aligned citizens may overlook cases affecting ideological opponents.

Social Segmentation

Fragmentation along lines of class, religion, and geography ensures that individual injustices are compartmentalized and seldom gain broader traction.

Media Mediation

High-profile, dramatized cases get attention; routine or less sensational instances remain invisible. Public focus becomes episodic and selective.

Distance creates a perception that injustice is exceptional rather than systemic.

II. Cultural and Cognitive Mechanisms of Silence

Fear and Risk Aversion

Speaking out can feel risky. Individuals worry about social, economic, or legal repercussions if they challenge powerful institutions.

Normalization of Authority

Repeated exposure to state-sanctioned narratives produces habituation: extraordinary claims about security threats begin to seem routine, and oversight feels optional.

Bystander Effect

People assume others will act, or believe that responsibility lies elsewhere, reducing individual engagement.

The result is inertia and passive consent.

III. Political Reinforcement of Passivity

Fear as a Political Tool

Election cycles exploit public anxiety, discouraging scrutiny of security operations. Citizens may prioritize perceived safety over critical inquiry.

Incentive Misalignment

Voters rarely reward oversight; they reward visible action and messaging that aligns with their concerns. Politicians and bureaucrats respond accordingly.

De-prioritization of Rights

Structural rights violations are tolerated because they lack immediate electoral consequences. Distal injustice is treated as abstract.

Political incentives silence the majority indirectly.

IV. Media and the Reproduction of Silence

Selective Amplification

Sensational stories are covered intensively; systemic failures without drama are under-reported.

Narrative Closure

Media cycles reward early framing and rapid attention, discouraging ongoing follow-up. Once a story fades, collective memory fades with it.

Individual Disconnection

Audiences consume episodic reporting, developing empathy for individuals but not systems. Structural patterns remain unexamined.

Media thus compounds societal distance.

V. The Moral Costs of Inattention

Collateral Harm

The burden of fighting injustice falls disproportionately on affected families, community advocates, and a few dedicated journalists.

Institutional Reinforcement

Lack of societal pressure allows investigative shortcuts, coercion, and procedural laxity to continue unchecked.

Cultural Entrenchment

Repeated silence normalizes the treatment of marginalized populations as peripheral to justice, creating intergenerational impact.

Indifference becomes an enabler.

VI. Case Studies: Silence and Its Consequences

Documented cases illustrate patterns:

- families fight for years against wrongful accusations, while broader society remains unaware
- journalists uncover systemic lapses but face limited public engagement
- judicial corrections arrive after prolonged social and personal damage

In each instance, absence of widespread attention allows structural flaws to persist.

VII. Mechanisms for Breaking Silence

Education and Awareness

Broad civic literacy programs contextualize systemic issues beyond individual anecdotes.

Media Accountability

Encouraging investigative depth, ongoing coverage, and public discussion of rights issues.

Civil Society Mobilization

Coalitions, NGOs, and legal aid organizations can translate episodic outrage into sustained advocacy.

Participatory Oversight

Community monitoring of law enforcement, public hearings, and citizen reporting channels.

Engagement requires structured opportunity and accessible pathways.

VIII. Psychological and Cultural Recalibration

Empathy Expansion

Storytelling that bridges distance can humanize marginalized experiences.

Systemic Framing

Education and discourse that emphasize patterns, rather than individual cases, foster long-term attention.

Normative Pressure

Social recognition for advocacy, whistleblowing, and accountability work can counteract risk aversion.

Shifting the collective mindset is central to breaking inertia.

IX. Legal and Human Rights Strategies

Transparency Mandates

Public access to investigation timelines, charges, and judicial reasoning increases collective visibility.

Institutional Feedback Loops

Mechanisms for civil society to provide input on ongoing cases promote proactive engagement.

Accountability Structures

Regular audits and independent reporting of systemic failures reinforce public attention and moral responsibility.

X. Sustaining Engagement Beyond Outrage

Long-Term Campaigns

Single-incident awareness is insufficient; advocacy must maintain attention across years and cycles.

Resource Support

Empowering citizens with tools—legal literacy, digital platforms, and research access—enables sustained participation.

Cultural Narratives

Societies that value oversight, empathy, and rights create environments where silence is socially costly.

Sustained engagement converts concern into systemic change.

Conclusion: Silence Is Not Neutral

The persistence of flawed investigations, coerced confessions, sensationalized reporting, and rights violations is not simply a product of institutional failure—it is also maintained by societal distance. When the majority remains silent, injustice can persist largely unchallenged, allowing systemic flaws to calcify and reproduce.

Breaking this silence requires both structural reforms and cultural transformation: education, media accountability, civic empowerment, and participatory mechanisms. Societies that remain passive implicitly condone what they do not challenge. Conversely, active engagement—whether through legal, journalistic, or civic channels—ensures that injustice is neither invisible nor inevitable.

Silence is a choice, and like all choices, it shapes the system. To address systemic injustice, the majority cannot remain spectators.

27: Legal Safeguards First

Bail Reform and Stricter Evidence Requirements

Introduction: Rights before Expediency

Across the preceding chapters, patterns have emerged: investigative shortcuts, politically useful arrests, sensational media coverage, and systemic silence all converge to produce wrongful prosecutions, extended pre-trial detention, and enduring social stigma. One consistent thread is the **lack of legal safeguards designed to prevent harm before it occurs**. Courts can correct mistakes post hoc, families can fight back, and journalists can highlight failures—but these are responses to harm, not prevention.

This chapter examines **legal safeguards as proactive mechanisms**—tools that prioritize individual rights, strengthen evidence standards, and reduce the systemic pressures that reward expediency over accuracy. It focuses on two interlinked areas: bail reform and stricter evidence requirements. Drawing on human rights law, comparative legal frameworks, investigative reporting, and case studies, the chapter presents reform proposals grounded in both principle and practical feasibility.

I. The Bail Paradox: Pre-Trial Detention as De Facto Punishment

Detention vs. Liberty

Bail, in theory, balances risk of flight or repeat offense with the presumption of innocence. In practice, systemic delays, political pressure, and institutional incentives transform pre-trial detention into prolonged punishment.

Disproportionate Impact

Marginalized individuals often lack resources to secure release. Wealth, education, and social capital become informal determinants of liberty.

The Cycle of Delay

Detention perpetuates case inertia: limited access to lawyers, inability to gather evidence, and weakened defense capacity increase the likelihood of prolonged trial and institutional momentum.

Bail thus operates less as a safeguard than as a mechanism of control.

II. Comparative Approaches to Bail Reform

International Standards

Human rights law emphasizes the **right to liberty**, presumption of innocence, and judicial discretion in setting conditions. UN Basic Principles on the Role of Lawyers and ICCPR provisions provide benchmarks.

Jurisdictional Innovations

Several jurisdictions have implemented reforms:

- **Conditional Release Programs**: Supervised release instead of default detention
- **Prompt Judicial Review**: Regular hearing timelines to prevent indefinite pre-trial custody
- **Financial Neutrality**: Bail decisions based on risk, not wealth

Evidence suggests these mechanisms reduce unnecessary detention without compromising security.

III. Stricter Evidence Requirements: Beyond Confession and Assumption

Confession and Coercion

Chapters 23 and 28 highlight the systemic reliance on confessions, sometimes extracted under duress, to justify arrests and sustain cases. Courts reject coerced evidence, but too often after prolonged detention.

Digital Misinterpretation

Chapter 24 documented how online activity, messaging, or social media posts are misread as criminal intent. Without rigorous evidentiary standards, innocent behavior is criminalized.

Physical and Forensic Evidence

Courts demand corroboration, chain-of-custody verification, and independent testing, but investigations sometimes treat such standards as secondary to narrative expediency.

Stricter evidence requirements would align investigative practice with legal principle.

IV. Legal Mechanisms to Enforce Evidence Standards

Pre-Charge Review

Judicial or independent review panels to assess sufficiency before formal charges

Disclosure Mandates

Timely and complete sharing of all evidence, including exculpatory material

Evidentiary Audits

Randomized case audits to identify investigative shortcuts, bias, or reliance on uncorroborated confessions

Expert Oversight

Mandatory review of forensic methods and digital evidence interpretation

By institutionalizing scrutiny at the outset, these mechanisms prevent weak cases from gaining momentum.

V. Intersection of Bail and Evidence

Pre-trial detention without strong evidence compounds harm:

- weak evidence prolongs detention
- detention reduces capacity to mount a defense
- institutional incentives reward visible arrest, regardless of evidentiary quality

Aligning bail decisions with evidence strength ensures liberty is not compromised by investigatory expedience.

VI. Institutional and Cultural Challenges

Resistance from Enforcement Agencies

Incentive structures reward arrests, not restraint. Early release or weak charges may be perceived as institutional failure.

Political Pressure

High-profile cases intersect with elections and security narratives, discouraging judicial leniency or skepticism.

Resource Limitations

Implementing pre-charge reviews, audits, and compliance monitoring requires investment and training.

Legal reform must anticipate and address these constraints.

VII. Human Rights Perspectives

Proportionality and Necessity

Bail restrictions must adhere to proportionality: only detention necessary to prevent flight, interference, or threat to society is permissible.

Equality before the Law

Reforms must reduce socio-economic bias, ensuring that indigent defendants are not disproportionately detained.

Preventive Justice vs. Reactive Remedy

A system that prevents harm through safeguards reduces reliance on retrospective remedies such as post-acquittal relief or moral vindication.

VIII. Judicial Role in Safeguard Enforcement

Proactive Oversight

Judges can insist on evidence sufficiency before approving detention or charge progression

Standards for Detention Review

Regular, structured evaluation of cases in custody to prevent prolonged deprivation

Encouragement of Legal Representation

Facilitating access to counsel during pre-trial proceedings strengthens the protective function of safeguards

IX. Case Studies: Where Safeguards Worked

Documented instances show that when courts enforce bail prudence and evidentiary standards:

- cases collapse faster when evidence is insufficient
- unnecessary detention is avoided
- investigative rigor improves due to early oversight

These examples highlight both feasibility and impact.

X. Recommendations for a Safeguard-Centric System

1. Bail Reform

- Presumption in favor of liberty
- Non-monetary conditions and supervised release
- Time-bound judicial review cycles

2. Evidence-Based Charge Decisions

- Pre-charge judicial review panels
- Mandatory disclosure of all materials

- Independent assessment of digital, forensic, and testimonial evidence

3. Training and Institutional Culture

- Continuous education on human rights, evidentiary standards, and procedural integrity
- Recognition and reward systems aligned with accuracy, not arrest counts

4. Monitoring and Transparency

- Public reporting of detention statistics, acquittals, and case withdrawals
- Feedback mechanisms for systemic evaluation

These measures collectively shift the system from reaction to prevention.

Conclusion: Safeguards as First Principles

Legal safeguards—particularly in bail and evidence standards—are not optional extras; they are **frontline defenses against systemic injustice**. By ensuring that detention is justified, evidence is robust, and procedural rights are protected, safeguards mitigate the human cost of investigative haste, political expediency, media sensationalism, and societal silence.

Putting safeguards first reorients the justice system toward **prevention rather than post hoc correction**, protecting both individuals and institutions. When law prioritizes liberty and accuracy, the cumulative effects of systemic pressure, public fear, and media amplification can be balanced, creating a more resilient, fair, and credible legal ecosystem.

28: Independent Review of Investigations

External Oversight of Terror Investigations

Introduction: Beyond Internal Accountability

Chapters preceding this one have systematically documented how political pressure, institutional incentives, media amplification, and societal silence shape terror investigations. Each dynamic interacts to produce weak cases, wrongful detentions, and prolonged pre-trial suffering. While legal safeguards like bail reform and stricter evidence requirements are crucial, they operate largely within the existing system. When the system itself is incentivized toward expediency, **internal safeguards are often insufficient.**

This chapter examines the role and necessity of **independent external review mechanisms**—oversight bodies, ombudsmen, and specialized commissions that can monitor, evaluate, and correct investigative practice outside the chain of command. Drawing on comparative law, investigative journalism, and human rights research, it analyzes how external scrutiny can restore procedural integrity, improve evidence quality, and reinforce public trust.

I. The Case for Independent Oversight

Limitations of Internal Review

Internal audits often fail due to:

- hierarchical deference
- career incentives favoring visible action over accuracy
- political influence

Without independent actors, errors and abuses may persist unnoticed or unaddressed.

Benefits of External Review

Independent review can:

- ensure procedural compliance and evidentiary rigor
- identify systemic patterns rather than isolated failures
- offer recommendations insulated from immediate political or career pressures

Oversight becomes both corrective and preventive.

II. Models of External Oversight

International Examples

- **United Kingdom**: Independent Office for Police Conduct (IOPC) reviews serious complaints and misconduct
- **Canada**: Civilian review boards oversee certain law enforcement actions, particularly in high-risk operations
- **South Africa**: Independent Police Investigative Directorate investigates serious crimes, including anti-terror enforcement

These models demonstrate feasibility, credibility, and public acceptance.

Key Features

1. Structural independence from agencies under review
2. Statutory authority to access files, evidence, and personnel
3. Mandated reporting and transparency requirements
4. Advisory or binding recommendations for reform

III. Mechanisms for Terror-Specific Oversight

Terror investigations present unique challenges:

- national security and secrecy concerns
- politically sensitive cases
- complex inter-agency coordination

Effective oversight may include:

- specialized review panels with security clearance
- liaison offices to balance secrecy with accountability
- protocols for evaluating classified evidence without compromising rights

Oversight design must reconcile security with transparency.

IV. Procedural Implementation

Case Selection

Not all investigations need external review. Criteria might include:

- high-profile terror allegations
- prolonged pre-trial detention
- cases involving marginalized communities

Timing and Scope

Reviews can be periodic (quarterly, annually) and case-specific. They may assess:

- investigative methodology
- evidence handling
- adherence to human rights standards

- alignment with legal safeguards

Enforcement Powers

Recommendations can be:

- advisory, to guide policy and practice
- binding, requiring corrective action or retraining

Mechanisms must be credible and actionable.

V. Preventive vs. Corrective Functions

Preventive Oversight

- early detection of flawed procedures
- discouragement of coercion or procedural shortcuts
- reinforcement of investigative rigor from the outset

Corrective Oversight

- identification of errors post-arrest or post-charge
- recommendations for case review or dismissal
- facilitation of accountability without waiting for court reversals

Both functions complement legal safeguards.

VI. Case Studies: Successes and Lessons

Investigations subject to independent review have shown:

- reduction in wrongful detentions
- increased compliance with evidence standards

- improved inter-agency coordination
- enhanced public confidence in justice processes

Failures often occur when review bodies lack independence, authority, or resources.

VII. Integration with Judicial and Legal Safeguards

Independent oversight reinforces other protective measures:

- aligns with bail and pre-charge review by assessing case strength
- complements evidence requirements by auditing methodology and corroboration
- strengthens procedural integrity when families or civil society lack capacity

Oversight is thus part of a **holistic system**.

VIII. Addressing Political and Institutional Resistance

Challenges include:

- reluctance from agencies fearing scrutiny
- political pressure to prioritize public perception over accuracy
- resource constraints

Mitigation strategies:

- statutory protection for review bodies
- clear mandate and independent funding

- public reporting to maintain accountability
- structured engagement with agencies to build compliance culture

Institutional acceptance is critical for effectiveness.

IX. Transparency and Public Trust

Public confidence in justice requires visible accountability. Independent oversight contributes by:

- publishing aggregate reports, trends, and reforms
- providing accessible summaries of systemic issues
- signaling that rights and fairness are institutional priorities

Transparency also counteracts societal silence and media distortion.

X. Recommendations for Effective External Oversight

1. **Structural Independence**: Legal separation from agencies under review
2. **Adequate Authority**: Access to files, personnel, and classified evidence under safeguards
3. **Mandated Reporting**: Public-facing reports detailing trends, patterns, and recommendations
4. **Integration with Legal Safeguards**: Complementing bail reform, evidence standards, and judicial oversight
5. **Capacity Building**: Training, resources, and technical expertise to evaluate complex terror investigations
6. **Preventive and Corrective Roles**: Monitoring ongoing investigations and reviewing completed cases to detect

systemic weaknesses

Oversight must be proactive, continuous, and credible.

Conclusion: Embedding Accountability in the System

Independent external review transforms accountability from a reactive, episodic process into a **permanent structural feature**. By auditing procedures, evidence, and rights compliance, these mechanisms prevent systemic errors, protect vulnerable populations, and restore public trust. When combined with bail reform, stricter evidence standards, and societal engagement, independent oversight closes critical gaps in the justice ecosystem.

In essence, external review ensures that terror investigations serve not only security objectives, but also the **principles of fairness, legality, and human rights**. It represents the final, essential layer in a multi-faceted system designed to prevent injustice before it can take root.

29: Hold actors accountable for wrongful prosecution

This chapter examines mechanisms to **hold actors accountable for wrongful prosecution**, exploring legal, procedural, and institutional frameworks that can deter fabrication, poor investigation, and abuse of process. Drawing on investigative reporting, human rights law, comparative legal practice, and case studies, it outlines strategies to balance deterrence, fairness, and the operational realities of law enforcement.

I. The Nature of Wrongful Prosecution

Forms of Misconduct

1. **Fabrication of Evidence** – deliberately creating or altering material to support a false charge
2. **Coerced Confessions** – obtaining statements under duress, threat, or intimidation
3. **Negligent Investigation** – ignoring exculpatory evidence, failing to verify claims, or misinterpreting digital/physical evidence
4. **Procedural Lapses** – failure to follow due process, disclosure obligations, or proper chain-of-custody procedures

These behaviors can be intentional or systemic, but both result in grave human and societal harm.

Consequences

- prolonged pre-trial detention
- criminalization of innocent activity

- reputational damage and social stigma
- erosion of public trust in law enforcement and judiciary

Accountability mechanisms are necessary to prevent recurrence.

II. Existing Accountability Mechanisms

Internal Disciplinary Processes

Agencies may conduct internal investigations, leading to reprimands, suspension, or dismissal. Limitations include:

- hierarchical bias
- conflict of interest
- lack of public transparency

Judicial Remedies

Courts can order acquittals, compensation, or procedural reforms but typically cannot impose sanctions on investigators or prosecutors.

Civil Liability

Victims may file civil suits, but litigation is expensive, prolonged, and often inaccessible to marginalized families.

These mechanisms rarely function as systemic deterrents.

III. Comparative Legal Approaches

United Kingdom

- **Criminal Proceedings Against Officials**: Law enforcement personnel can face charges for fabricating evidence or perverting the course of justice

- **Independent Oversight**: Offices like IOPC provide public accountability and recommend prosecution

United States

- **Brady Violations**: Suppression of exculpatory evidence can trigger both civil liability and professional sanctions
- **Prosecutorial Discipline Boards**: Attorneys may be sanctioned for misconduct

South Africa

- Independent investigative directorates can refer misconduct for criminal prosecution

Effective systems combine external oversight, professional regulation, and legal sanction.

IV. Proposed Accountability Mechanisms

1. Criminal Sanctions for Misconduct

- **Perverting the Course of Justice**: Clear statutes covering fabrication, coercion, and negligent investigation
- **Proportional Penalties**: Fines, dismissal, or imprisonment depending on intent and harm

2. Professional Accountability

- Licensing bodies for prosecutors and investigators with powers to suspend, retrain, or revoke credentials
- Mandatory reporting of disciplinary actions to maintain transparency

3. Civil Remedies

- Compensation funds for victims of wrongful prosecution
- Streamlined litigation processes for indigent defendants
- Ability to recover costs associated with legal defense, lost income, and rehabilitation

4. Institutional Safeguards

- Policies linking investigative outcomes to oversight review rather than promotion alone
- Periodic audits of investigative units for procedural compliance
- Public reporting of collapsed cases to identify patterns

Accountability should be **multi-layered** to address individual, professional, and systemic failures.

V. Challenges to Implementation

Political Resistance

High-profile cases or politically sensitive investigations may shield responsible actors from scrutiny.

Resource Constraints

Investigating misconduct, especially retroactively, requires personnel, expertise, and funding.

Cultural Resistance

Institutional cultures emphasizing loyalty and reputation over accuracy can impede enforcement.

Effective accountability must navigate these challenges with statutory clarity and procedural independence.

VI. Preventive Impact of Accountability

- **Behavioral Deterrence**: Awareness of potential sanctions encourages adherence to evidence standards and procedural norms
- **Improved Investigation Quality**: Independent review combined with accountability fosters rigorous, methodical practice
- **Restoration of Trust**: Public confidence improves when misconduct is addressed transparently and proportionally

VII. Integration with Oversight and Safeguards

Accountability is most effective when coupled with:

- bail and evidence-based legal safeguards (Chapter 31)
- independent external review mechanisms (Chapter 32)
- media transparency and civic oversight (Chapters 29–30)

The combination ensures that misconduct is both **prevented and corrected**, while preserving operational effectiveness.

VIII. Case Studies: Lessons Learned

- In cases where misconduct was prosecuted, future investigations in the same units improved compliance and procedural rigor
- Jurisdictions with combined oversight and sanction mechanisms show lower rates of wrongful detention

- Victim-centered compensation programs restore social and economic stability, enhancing legitimacy

These examples illustrate the **practical and ethical benefits** of enforcing accountability.

IX. Recommendations for a Robust Accountability Framework

1. **Statutory Clarity**: Explicit laws defining misconduct and associated penalties
2. **Independent Investigative Authority**: External review bodies empowered to refer cases for criminal or professional sanction
3. **Integrated Oversight**: Coordination with courts, regulatory boards, and civil society
4. **Transparency and Reporting**: Public disclosure of disciplinary actions and case outcomes
5. **Preventive Culture**: Incentive alignment to reward thorough, evidence-based investigations over speed or publicity

These measures create a deterrent effect while respecting due process and operational necessity.

Conclusion: Accountability as a Pillar of Justice

Punishing wrongful prosecution is not only a moral imperative; it is essential to **breaking cycles of investigative failure, social harm, and public distrust**. Accountability complements legal safeguards, oversight, and civic engagement, ensuring that investigations serve justice rather than expediency or political interest. When officers, prosecutors, and institutions understand that misconduct carries consequences, the system prioritizes accuracy, fairness, and human rights.

Accountability is the final, reinforcing layer in a multi-dimensional framework for reform—without it, safeguards, oversight, and civic vigilance risk being insufficient to prevent recurring injustice.

30: Media Ethics & Naming Protocols

Avoiding Religion or Community Mention Before Conviction

Introduction: Responsible Reporting in Sensitive Cases

Media coverage is a central force shaping public perception of terror-related investigations. As previous chapters have shown, sensational reporting, selective amplification, and framing biases can magnify fear, pressure institutions, and stigmatize innocent individuals and communities. Among the most consequential missteps is the **premature association of accused individuals with religion, ethnicity, or community**, which can reinforce stereotypes, fuel discrimination, and exacerbate social harm.

This chapter examines the ethical and legal imperatives for **naming protocols and responsible reporting**, balancing public interest with the presumption of innocence. Drawing on human rights law, journalism standards, and investigative analysis, it proposes practical reforms for ethical media practice in reporting terror cases.

I. The Problem: Identity Framing Before Conviction

Social and Psychological Impact

- Associating religion or community with criminal allegations reinforces **prejudice and social exclusion**.
- Families and neighbors of the accused often face **collective stigmatization**.
- Public perception can become skewed, making **fair trial and**

jury impartiality difficult to maintain.

Case Examples

Investigative reports have documented scenarios where:

- Muslim individuals accused of terror activities were highlighted with religious identifiers in headlines and broadcasts
- Communities experienced protests, harassment, or social ostracism before any conviction
- Media framing influenced political and institutional narratives

The consequence is **prejudgment in the public sphere**, which can indirectly affect institutional and judicial behavior.

II. International Standards and Guidelines

Human Rights Framework

- **ICCPR Article 14**: Guarantees presumption of innocence
- **UN Human Rights Principles**: Emphasize privacy, dignity, and fair trial rights

Media Codes of Conduct

- International Press Institute (IPI) and Reporters Without Borders (RSF) advocate **non-disclosure of religion or ethnicity unless directly relevant to the story**
- Emphasis on **context, accuracy, and balance**, particularly in sensitive security cases

These frameworks establish ethical and legal baselines for reporting.

III. Risks of Naming Protocol Violations

Legal Risks

- Defamation and libel suits
- Interference with ongoing investigations
- Potential violations of privacy and data protection laws

Social Risks

- Stigmatization of communities
- Escalation of communal tensions
- Erosion of public trust in both media and legal institutions

Institutional Risks

- Pressure on law enforcement to act in line with media-driven narratives
- Politically charged reinforcement of investigative bias

Failure to follow naming protocols has wide-ranging consequences beyond individual harm.

IV. Ethical Principles for Media Practice

1. **Presumption of Innocence**: Avoid implying guilt prior to conviction
2. **Minimal Identifiers**: Limit personal information to what is legally and publicly relevant
3. **Avoidance of Religion, Caste, or Community Labels**: Unless contextually essential

4. **Contextual Reporting**: Provide background, uncertainty, and judicial process updates
5. **Transparent Corrections**: Immediately address errors or premature identification

Adhering to these principles ensures reporting respects both human rights and social cohesion.

V. Naming Protocol Implementation

Editorial Guidelines

- Standard operating procedures for sensitive cases
- Mandatory review of language, images, and identifiers before publication
- Training for journalists in rights-based reporting

Legal Coordination

- Liaison with judicial authorities to verify public disclosure guidelines
- Awareness of ongoing investigations and sealed case restrictions

Digital Media Considerations

- Social media amplification requires pre-publication controls
- Use of anonymized reporting and delayed naming protocols to prevent viral misinformation

VI. Balancing Public Interest and Individual Rights

Situations Requiring Identity Disclosure

- When identity is critical for public safety (e.g., wanted persons)
- When the individual voluntarily discloses identity
- Court-authorized publication after due process

Avoiding Unnecessary Harm

- Even legally permissible disclosure should be evaluated against social consequences
- Editors must weigh journalistic impact against potential stigmatization

Responsible reporting ensures public knowledge without causing unjust harm.

VII. Case Studies: Lessons from Missteps

- Cases where community identifiers were highlighted before conviction show **long-term stigma and social disruption**
- Corrective measures such as post-acquittal media statements were often underreported, leaving public perception skewed
- Investigative journalism that adhered to naming protocols maintained credibility, trust, and minimized social tension

These examples underscore the importance of proactive ethical protocols.

VIII. Training and Institutional Measures

- Mandatory workshops on rights-based reporting
- Creation of in-house ethical review committees
- Scenario-based training on sensitive terror cases
- Periodic audits of reporting practices and adherence to naming protocols

Education reinforces systemic commitment to ethical journalism.

IX. Policy and Regulatory Recommendations

1. **Statutory Guidelines**: Enact laws or regulations mandating non-disclosure of religion/community prior to conviction
2. **Press Councils and Regulatory Bodies**: Monitor compliance, issue directives, and provide guidance
3. **Corrective Mechanisms**: Require prominent, timely corrections for premature or inaccurate identification
4. **Collaboration with Law Enforcement**: Guidelines on permissible disclosures during ongoing investigations
5. **Public Awareness**: Educate citizens on responsible media consumption and the presumption of innocence

These measures create both ethical and enforceable norms.

X. Conclusion: Preserving Fairness and Social Cohesion

Naming protocols are not simply technical rules—they are **ethical, legal, and social safeguards**. By avoiding religion, caste, or community identifiers before conviction, media organizations uphold the presumption of innocence, protect marginalized communities, and reduce undue social harm. Ethical reporting strengthens both justice and democracy, ensuring that public discourse reflects verified fact rather than sensationalized prejudice.

When combined with legal safeguards, independent oversight, and accountability mechanisms, adherence to media ethics and naming protocols forms a **comprehensive protective layer**, preventing both individual and systemic injustice.

31: Community Legal Literacy

Education on Rights during Arrest, Interrogation, and Trial

Introduction: Empowering the Vulnerable

While previous chapters have addressed systemic failures—from investigative shortcuts to media sensationalism, pre-trial detention, and lack of accountability—a recurring factor is the **knowledge gap among ordinary citizens about their legal rights**. Families and communities often lack understanding of procedural safeguards, rights during arrest, interrogation protocols, and courtroom procedures. This knowledge deficit exacerbates vulnerability, prolongs detention, diminishes defense effectiveness, and compounds social stigma.

This chapter explores **community legal literacy** as a vital preventive tool. It examines strategies for educating the public, empowering marginalized populations, and embedding legal awareness into everyday life. Drawing on human rights research, investigative journalism, and legal analysis, the chapter proposes a structured approach to equipping citizens with actionable knowledge to navigate the criminal justice system.

I. The Knowledge Gap

Arrest and Detention

Many individuals and families are unaware of:

- the right to be informed of charges
- the right to legal counsel
- the right to remain silent and avoid self-incrimination
- procedural timelines for filing bail and challenging detention

This ignorance leaves suspects vulnerable to coercion and extended pre-trial detention.

Interrogation Practices

- Uninformed individuals may inadvertently provide statements that are misinterpreted as incriminating
- Vulnerable populations, including youth and marginalized communities, are particularly susceptible to intimidation
- Awareness of rights to counsel and recording of interrogations can prevent misuse

Trial Procedures

- Misunderstanding court process, evidence presentation, and testimony rights hinders defense participation
- Families may fail to challenge procedural lapses, disclosure omissions, or weak prosecutorial claims

Knowledge gaps create both **immediate harm** and **long-term social consequences.**

II. The Case for Legal Literacy

Empowerment and Agency

Educated citizens are better equipped to:

- assert their rights
- participate meaningfully in their defense
- hold authorities accountable

Preventive Effect

When communities understand legal thresholds, coercive practices and procedural shortcuts are less likely to succeed.

Reinforcing Systemic Checks

Legal literacy complements safeguards such as bail reform, stricter evidence standards, and oversight mechanisms. An informed citizenry magnifies the impact of these systemic reforms.

III. Methods for Community Legal Education

Grassroots Workshops

- Conducted by NGOs, bar associations, or legal aid organizations
- Focused on practical rights during arrest, interrogation, and trial
- Use of interactive, scenario-based learning for retention and relevance

School and College Programs

- Incorporating legal literacy modules into curricula
- Youth-focused education on digital rights, online messaging, and social media conduct
- Simulation of courtroom procedures and mock trials

Digital Platforms

- Accessible online resources, video tutorials, and interactive guides
- Mobile applications with legal information tailored to

specific regions and communities
- Social media campaigns to disseminate rights-oriented content

Community Centers and Libraries

- Localized legal resource hubs with trained volunteers and materials in multiple languages
- Regular open sessions for Q&A and case-specific guidance

IV. Focused Topics for Literacy Programs

1. **Rights During Arrest**
    - Right to information, legal counsel, and silent reflection
    - Right against unlawful detention
2. **Interrogation Safeguards**
    - Right to refuse self-incriminating statements
    - Presence of counsel during questioning
    - Documentation of interrogation proceedings
3. **Trial Rights**
    - Access to all evidence, including exculpatory material
    - Cross-examination and procedural remedies
    - Understanding bail, appeals, and acquittal procedures
4. **Digital Conduct Awareness**
    - Risks of online activity misinterpreted as intent
    - Secure communication practices and digital evidence literacy

Comprehensive literacy programs integrate all stages of the justice process.

V. Challenges in Legal Literacy Implementation

Socio-Economic Barriers

- Poverty, illiteracy, and geographic remoteness limit access to education programs

Cultural and Linguistic Diversity

- Materials must be culturally sensitive and available in local languages
- Outreach must address traditional hierarchies and community dynamics

Resource and Institutional Constraints

- Sustained funding, trained personnel, and institutional support are necessary for effective programs

VI. Case Studies: Successes and Lessons

- Community workshops led by legal aid organizations reduced instances of coerced confessions and prolonged detention
- Digital campaigns in multiple languages increased awareness of rights among youth in high-risk areas
- Partnerships between bar associations and civil society groups empowered families to navigate trials more effectively

Lessons demonstrate that **targeted, accessible, and practical education can meaningfully reduce vulnerability**.

VII. Integrating Legal Literacy with Systemic Safeguards

- Literacy complements bail reforms by enabling timely filing and advocacy
- Knowledge of evidence standards empowers citizens to challenge weak investigations
- Awareness of oversight mechanisms strengthens external review and accountability

Legal literacy is not a substitute for systemic reform but **a force multiplier**, ensuring that reforms reach the individuals they are designed to protect.

VIII. Policy and Programmatic Recommendations

1. **Nationwide Legal Literacy Initiatives**: Government-supported campaigns in collaboration with NGOs and bar councils
2. **Mandatory Curriculum Inclusion**: Introduce rights education from secondary school onwards
3. **Localized Resource Centers**: Community hubs with trained volunteers and multilingual materials
4. **Digital Access and Apps**: Mobile-first approaches for remote and underserved areas
5. **Evaluation and Feedback Mechanisms**: Continuous assessment to measure effectiveness and adapt methods

These strategies ensure that legal literacy is **sustained, measurable, and accessible**.

IX. Long-Term Social Impact

- Reduction in wrongful detention and coerced confessions
- Empowered communities capable of engaging with law enforcement and judicial systems
- Strengthened trust between citizens and institutions
- Mitigation of social stigma through proactive knowledge and rights assertion

Legal literacy transforms passive vulnerability into **active, informed participation.**

Conclusion: Literacy as a Pillar of Justice

Community legal literacy is both a **protective and transformative tool**. By educating citizens about their rights during arrest, interrogation, and trial, societies can reduce the human cost of investigative shortcuts, prevent coercion, and improve judicial outcomes. Legal literacy enhances the effectiveness of safeguards, oversight, and accountability mechanisms discussed in prior chapters. Ultimately, an informed public becomes a **partner in justice**, capable of defending both individual rights and systemic integrity.

32: Data Transparency

Public Reporting of Arrests vs Convictions by Law and Religion

Introduction: Illuminating Systemic Patterns

Across previous chapters, the manuscript has explored the intersections of investigative shortcuts, media framing, societal silence, pre-trial detention, oversight failures, and legal illiteracy. Yet one critical layer remains underdeveloped in practice: **systematic, disaggregated data transparency**. Without robust public reporting, patterns of wrongful arrest, bias, and disproportionality remain invisible. Policymakers, civil society, journalists, and affected communities lack the evidence necessary to drive reform.

This chapter examines the imperative of **public reporting of arrests and convictions**, disaggregated by legal framework and community identity, including religion, caste, and other relevant markers. It explores methodologies, ethical considerations, global best practices, and policy recommendations for data transparency, emphasizing its role as both **diagnostic and preventive** in ensuring justice.

I. The Problem: Invisible Patterns

Discrepancy between Arrests and Convictions

- Investigative studies show that large numbers of arrests do not translate into convictions
- Delays, weak evidence, and coercion contribute to systemic inefficiency
- Public discourse often assumes arrest equates to guilt,

obscuring reality

Lack of Disaggregated Data

- Aggregate statistics mask disproportionate targeting of marginalized communities
- Absence of religion, caste, or community indicators in public data limits scrutiny of systemic bias
- Journalistic narratives, without quantitative backing, risk anecdotal overgeneralization

The invisibility of data undermines accountability and reform.

II. Legal and Ethical Considerations

Privacy vs Public Interest

- Protecting individual identities while reporting aggregate statistics
- Avoiding re-traumatization or social harm from data disclosure
- Ensuring that reports illuminate systemic patterns without stigmatizing individuals

Human Rights Framework

- Transparency as a right and tool to promote equality (ICCPR, UN Principles on the Role of Lawyers)
- Legal requirement for impartiality and non-discrimination in reporting and enforcement

Responsible data practices balance transparency with ethical safeguards.

III. Global Best Practices

United Kingdom

- Ministry of Justice publishes annual statistics on arrests, prosecutions, and convictions, including breakdowns by ethnicity, religion, and socio-economic indicators
- Data informs policy, oversight, and media reporting

Canada

- Public Safety and Justice departments provide open-access crime data with demographic breakdowns
- Civil society uses data to identify disparities and recommend reforms

Australia

- Regular reporting on charges, outcomes, and demographic markers, accompanied by analysis to highlight potential bias

These examples demonstrate feasibility and public utility.

IV. Methodologies for Effective Reporting

Standardized Data Collection

- Consistent categories across jurisdictions (e.g., charges, outcomes, community identifiers)
- Clear protocols for law enforcement data entry and validation

Disaggregation Metrics

- Arrests and convictions by law (terror, criminal, civil) and by religion/community
- Temporal trends to detect changes over time
- Geographic breakdowns to identify hotspots of disproportionality

Independent Verification

- Oversight bodies or third-party audits to ensure accuracy and completeness
- Mechanisms for correcting errors or omissions

Robust methodology ensures credibility and actionable insights.

V. Analytical Uses of Transparent Data

Identifying Systemic Bias

- Compare arrest-to-conviction ratios across communities
- Examine correlation with investigative practices, political events, or media coverage
- Detect patterns of repeated targeting or procedural anomalies

Policy Evaluation

- Assess the impact of bail reforms, evidence safeguards, and oversight mechanisms
- Evaluate resource allocation and effectiveness of training programs

Civic Engagement

- Provide NGOs, journalists, and communities with empirical basis for advocacy
- Empower citizens with information for informed dialogue and participation

Data becomes a tool for accountability, not just record-keeping.

VI. Ethical Communication of Data

Aggregation and Anonymization

- Avoid reporting individual-level identifiers unless legally mandated
- Present data in ways that highlight systemic patterns, not stigmatize communities

Contextualization

- Include explanatory notes on investigative delays, legal thresholds, and case complexities
- Prevent misinterpretation by policymakers, media, or public

Transparency about Limitations

- Document data collection methods, coverage gaps, and potential biases
- Enable critical assessment and continuous improvement

Ethical communication preserves public trust and utility.

VII. Integration with Oversight and Safeguards

- Data transparency enhances independent review effectiveness (Chapter 32)
- Supports legal literacy efforts (Chapter 35) by providing tangible examples of rights application
- Strengthens media ethics by giving journalists verified, disaggregated facts rather than anecdotal narratives (Chapter 34)
- Complements accountability mechanisms for wrongful prosecution (Chapter 33)

Transparent data forms a backbone connecting systemic reforms.

VIII. Implementation Strategies

Legislative Mandates

- Require regular reporting on arrests, charges, and convictions
- Specify disaggregation by law and relevant identity markers

Institutional Protocols

- Standardized templates for law enforcement data entry
- Regular audits and independent verification

Public Access Platforms

- Online dashboards, downloadable datasets, and annual reports
- Interactive tools for trend analysis and visual representation

Civil Society Collaboration

- NGOs, academics, and journalists can analyze, disseminate, and contextualize data for public understanding

IX. Challenges and Mitigation

Data Accuracy and Completeness

- Training and quality control protocols for personnel
- Integration with oversight mechanisms to detect and correct errors

Political and Institutional Resistance

- Emphasize neutral, systemic benefit of data transparency
- Leverage public demand, judicial directives, and advocacy to enforce compliance

Ethical Dilemmas

- Ensure anonymization and aggregation prevent individual harm
- Independent ethics committees to review reporting standards

X. Conclusion: Transparency as Preventive Justice

Public reporting of arrests versus convictions, disaggregated by law and community, is more than a bureaucratic exercise. It is a **diagnostic, preventive, and corrective tool** that illuminates patterns of bias, informs policy, empowers civil society, and strengthens public trust. By making systemic outcomes visible, transparency transforms accountability from reactive to proactive, reinforcing legal safeguards, oversight, literacy, and ethical media practice.

In a system where investigative shortcuts, social silence, and media framing previously allowed injustice to persist, **data transparency is the lens that reveals patterns, empowers citizens, and drives reform**. It completes the 360-degree framework for evidence-based, rights-respecting, and solution-oriented justice outlined throughout this manuscript.

33: Reclaiming Citizenship

Security Must Respect Civil Liberties; Muslim ≠ Suspect

Introduction: Citizenship under Suspicion

Throughout this manuscript, the impact of flawed terror investigations on individuals, families, and communities has been traced across multiple layers: investigative shortcuts, political pressures, media sensationalism, social stigma, and systemic gaps in legal safeguards. A recurring theme emerges: **the presumption of suspicion assigned to Muslim citizens in the context of national security cases.** This chapter examines how security practices intersect with civil liberties, the rule of law, and citizenship rights, and it explores pathways to restore equitable recognition of citizenship without compromising security imperatives.

By integrating investigative reporting, human rights research, and legal analysis, this chapter situates the Muslim experience in the broader debate over **security versus civil liberties**, offering practical, solution-oriented strategies for reclaiming rights and reinforcing democratic norms.

I. The Problem: Citizenship Conditional on Suspicion

Historical and Societal Context

- Across multiple high-profile investigations, Muslim citizens have been disproportionately associated with terror activity
- This association persists regardless of evidence, often driven by media narratives, political expediency, and institutional

bias

- Families, communities, and individuals experience both **legal vulnerability and social exclusion**, including harassment, surveillance, and economic marginalization

Structural Impacts

- Extended pre-trial detention and wrongful prosecutions erode **legal equality**
- Social stigma reinforces communal alienation, affecting employment, education, and civic participation
- Fear of profiling diminishes trust in law enforcement and democratic institutions

These patterns highlight a gap between **formal citizenship rights** and the lived experience of Muslim communities.

II. Legal Foundations of Citizenship and Civil Liberties

Constitutional Guarantees

- Equality before the law and protection against discrimination (constitutional and human rights provisions)
- Right to liberty, due process, and presumption of innocence
- Freedom of religion, expression, and association

International Standards

- ICCPR Articles 2 and 26 emphasize equality and non-discrimination
- UN Human Rights Committee guidance underscores that security measures must **not target communities based on**

identity

Legal frameworks establish a baseline for **rights-respecting security practices.**

III. Security Practices That Undermine Citizenship

Profiling and Targeting

- Reliance on religion or community identity as an investigative heuristic
- Algorithmic or intelligence-based screening that disproportionately flags Muslim individuals
- Overemphasis on social media or online activity within specific communities

Consequences of Discrimination

- Wrongful arrests, detention, and harassment
- Disproportionate legal burden on marginalized populations
- Erosion of civic engagement and alienation from democratic processes

Systemic profiling undermines the core principle that **citizenship should be identity-neutral.**

IV. Media and Political Amplification

- Media narratives often link Muslim identity with threat, reinforcing public suspicion
- Political actors may leverage security fears for electoral gains, shaping policy and public perception

- The combination of media framing and political instrumentalization reinforces the cycle of conditional citizenship

V. Restoring Equitable Citizenship: Legal Strategies

Strengthening Presumption of Innocence

- Judicial enforcement of rights during arrest, interrogation, and trial (Chapters 31, 35)
- Monitoring of pre-trial detention to prevent identity-based targeting

Anti-Discrimination Safeguards

- Explicit legal protections against profiling based on religion or ethnicity
- Statutory remedies for wrongful detention or prosecution (Chapter 33)

Oversight Mechanisms

- Independent review of investigations to identify identity-based bias (Chapter 32)
- Transparent public reporting of arrests, prosecutions, and convictions disaggregated by community (Chapter 36)

Legal interventions can reclaim citizenship rights by embedding accountability and fairness into security practices.

VI. Social and Civic Interventions

Community Engagement

- Legal literacy programs targeting marginalized communities to reinforce rights awareness (Chapter 35)
- Collaboration with NGOs and civil society to monitor enforcement practices

Media Ethics

- Responsible reporting avoiding identity framing before conviction (Chapter 34)
- Public campaigns emphasizing individual guilt, not community identity

Civic Participation

- Encouraging engagement in democratic institutions despite prior suspicion
- Rehabilitating social status post-acquittal through visibility, advocacy, and support networks

Social interventions complement legal safeguards to **restore citizenship legitimacy**.

VII. Case Studies: Reclaiming Rights in Practice

- Post-acquittal reintegration initiatives highlight the importance of both legal and social rehabilitation
- Independent investigations correcting procedural errors reinforce trust in institutions

- Data-driven transparency demonstrates that arrests are not community-wide indictments, helping counter public prejudice

These examples show that **citizenship can be reaffirmed through deliberate structural, legal, and social measures.**

VIII. Policy Recommendations

1. **Explicit Anti-Profiling Policies**: Enforcement agencies must avoid identity-based heuristics in security operations
2. **Judicial Vigilance**: Courts must enforce presumption of innocence and scrutinize evidence for bias
3. **Community-Led Oversight**: Citizen and NGO participation in monitoring security operations
4. **Data Transparency and Public Reporting**: Aggregate statistics disaggregated by religion/community to detect systemic disparities
5. **Media Responsibility**: Ethical reporting protocols to prevent identity-linked stigmatization
6. **Legal Literacy Campaigns**: Educate communities on rights and procedural safeguards

Integrated implementation ensures that **security and citizenship rights are mutually reinforcing, not in conflict.**

IX. Long-Term Implications

- Reducing identity-based targeting restores social cohesion
- Trust in law enforcement and the justice system is strengthened
- Democratically enshrined rights gain practical, lived

expression
- Security practices become more precise, effective, and rights-compliant

Citizenship is reaffirmed when legal, social, and institutional systems treat individuals equitably, regardless of religion or background.

Conclusion: Citizenship as a Right, Not a Conditional Privilege

Muslim citizens, like all citizens, should enjoy **full rights and protections under the law**, without suspicion or prejudice based on identity. Security must operate within civil liberties, ensuring that investigative rigor does not morph into community-wide profiling. Reclaiming citizenship requires a **multi-layered approach**, combining legal safeguards, independent oversight, ethical media, community engagement, and transparency.

When identity ceases to dictate suspicion, the social contract is restored, democratic institutions gain legitimacy, and justice operates as a **universal, rather than conditional, entitlement**. Reclaiming citizenship is both a corrective measure for past injustices and a preventive framework for the future.

Conclusion: Justice, Rights, and Reform

Throughout this book, we have traced a comprehensive arc of the contemporary justice landscape, particularly as it intersects with terror investigations, systemic bias, and the lived experiences of marginalized communities. From flawed investigative practices and coercion to media sensationalism, social stigma, and institutional incentives, each chapter has exposed the multifaceted pressures that can compromise the principles of fairness, presumption of innocence, and human rights.

At the same time, the book is **solution-oriented and reform-driven**. It emphasizes legal safeguards, independent oversight, accountability mechanisms, media ethics, community legal literacy, data transparency, and the restoration of equitable citizenship. By interweaving investigative journalism, human rights research, and legal analysis, it presents a **360-degree approach**: diagnosing systemic failures, understanding social and political consequences, and proposing actionable reforms to create a justice ecosystem that is fair, transparent, and accountable.

The ultimate argument is clear: **security and civil liberties are not mutually exclusive**. With structured oversight, informed citizens, ethical media, and enforceable safeguards, societies can protect against terror while respecting the rights and dignity of all citizens. The reforms outlined here are not theoretical—they are practical, implementable, and necessary for sustaining democratic justice in complex, high-stakes environments.

About the Author

Fazal Abubakkar Esaf Known for his meticulous field research and incisive legal critique, Esaf combines **rigorous evidence-gathering with narrative clarity**, highlighting the human and societal impact of policy and institutional failure.

His work has consistently focused on the intersection of **law, security, and civil liberties**, with a particular emphasis on marginalized communities and vulnerable populations. Esaf's reporting and analysis have informed policy debates, guided advocacy efforts, and contributed to public understanding of complex legal and social dynamics. Through this book, he continues his commitment to **rights-based, solution-oriented investigative scholarship**, providing both a critical diagnosis and a roadmap for systemic reform.

Don't miss out!

Visit the website below and you can sign up to receive emails whenever Fazal Abubakkar Esaf publishes a new book. There's no charge and no obligation.

https://books2read.com/r/B-A-KTQWD-RVPZI

BOOKS 2 READ

Connecting independent readers to independent writers.

Did you love *Suspect by Default*? Then you should read *Beyond Division: Psychology, Strategy, and the Politics of Harmony*[1] by Fazal Abubakkar Esaf!

[2]

In India's complex sociopolitical landscape, Hindu-Muslim divisions have been both a tool and a consequence of political strategy. The present work is an analytical exploration of how such divisions are engineered, sustained, and internalized at multiple levels: individual, communal, and institutional.—this book diagnoses the mechanisms of division and offers practical strategies for counteraction.

The book moves from understanding the historical and psychological roots of communal polarization to examining mass psychology, systemic influences, internal community dynamics, and, ultimately, counter-strategies for resilience. Each chapter combines

---

1. https://books2read.com/u/3J7OPE
2. https://books2read.com/u/3J7OPE

empirical insights with solution-oriented recommendations, enabling readers to engage critically with the political landscape while exploring actionable interventions.

This book is intended for scholars, policymakers, civil society leaders, and citizens alike. It offers not only a diagnostic framework for understanding communal politics but also a roadmap for building strategic, ethical, and sustainable interventions.

Also by Fazal Abubakkar Esaf

Silent Streets
The Wind doesn't keep Diaries
Stress Free Teachers
Pardon My Cabinet
The Muslim Room You never Visited
Three Bullets,Two Bodies,One Lie
I Met You between Heartbeats
Chronicles from the Forbidden Future
The Garden within the House
The Garden within the House
The Silence Beneath the Soul
Meadow Days & Candlelight Nights
When Love withers in Silence
And Still, We Loved Again
Everyday Battles: Fight, Faith, Future
Love that lives in wounds
Monsoon Inside Room
Pure Joy Bonds
Nowhere to Belong
Voices in the Riddim
Loving You Was a War I Lost Beautifully
Map of You in Me
The Echo Within the Silence
Wolves Eat the Wind
Love Stories in the Language of Rain and Ruins

Nafs Unveiled: A Journey into the Healing Heart of the Soul
The Banana Leaf Was Still Warm
The Pandemic Diaries
Love in the Long Queue
Maps Left in Rain
Rumours from the Coconut Wireless
The Streets Between Us
Where the Sky Drinks the Sea
The Beautiful Lie We Live
Fingerprint of Crimes
Tides of Silence, Shores of Renewal
We Were a Poem with No Ending
He Loved Me in Parentheses
Whispers Between Walls
Khaki Reflection: voices from the uniform
Glass Shadows: Poems
River Without Source
Another Night with No Cigarettes
The Road North and Other Stories
Whispers Between Memory and the City
Reflections on Meaning and Suffering
The Psychology of Collective Tales
Footprints in the Monsoon Mist
The Inner Road of the Waking Man
Whispers and Wings
Between Concrete and Dust
India's Riots A People's Guide to History, Causes, and Healing.
Politics without Illusions
Lives Between Thought and Silence
Ordinary Dust, Living Stories
Stories of Memory, Identity, and Urban Lives
Rebuilding Muslim Economies
When the Azan Meets the Morning Sun

Where The City Leaves its Shadows
After the War: What Remains
Beyond Division: Psychology, Strategy, and the Politics of Harmony
The Refugee Experience
Muslims in Contemporary India
The Unsaid Lives of Enclosed Spaces
From Death to Truth
Narrative Residue
Whispers of the Courtyard
Echoes of the Human Soul
Quiet Truths
Ten Percent Human
Silent Pursuit
The Reflective Waters of the Heart
When No One Is Left
Maratha's Complete Art of Asymmetric War
Political Strategy Lessons from Maratha Commanders
Evidence Doesn't Always Cast Shadows
Invisible To Accountable
Lives of Incomplete People
The Last Question
Ghosts Were Never the Killers
Suspect by Default
Unopposed
Lives Misread
When Machines Learn To Feel
When Time Walked Slower

www.ingramcontent.com/pod-product-compliance
Lightning Source LLC
LaVergne TN
LVHW090355210926
848480LV00002B/344
9798233643095